WALLACE D. CHAPPELL

HIS
CONTINUED
WITNESS

Abingdon Press   New York   Nashville

SET UP, PRINTED, AND BOUND BY THE
PARTHENON PRESS, AT NASHVILLE,
TENNESSEE, UNITED STATES OF AMERICA

TO MY WIFE
MARY FRANCES

next to the Savior the dearest thing that ever happened to me

PREFACE

While applying the finishing touches to this manuscript, I was preaching in a Presbyterian Bible conference with my friend, Norman Hope, of Princeton University.

I told him that I considered the fundamental purpose of the Incarnation to be the indwelling Spirit. He replied that he would agree if the Crucifixion and Resurrection were not omitted. We certainly had no disagreement there for the Crucifixion and Resurrection are indeed the mountain peaks of the Gospels.

The book of Acts could rightly be called "The Acts of the Risen Lord," for it is he that is the Spirit within.

Luke begins the Acts of the Apostles by saying, "In the first book . . . I have dealt with all that Jesus began to do and teach." The book of Acts then is the continuing witness of Christ in the person and through the power of the Holy Spirit.

These simple sermons deal with experiences in the life of the early church and its leadership. They have a two-fold purpose: to induce a fresh consideration of this amazing volume by the Beloved Physician, and to exhort each of us to be a channel through which the Holy Spirit can flow.

—WALLACE D. CHAPPELL

CONTENTS

9

WAITING FOR THE PROMISE

While staying with them he charged them not to depart from Jerusalem, but to wait for the promise of the Father.
—ACTS 1:4

Frequently I gaze at a painting that is rich in tender pathos. A small boy is blowing bubbles and watching them disappear. There is a wistfulness about the little chap that is immediately noticeable. "Perhaps this bubble," he seems to be saying, "will not burst." But of course each one does.

11

And all that is left of this mite of sparkling foam, that seemed to promise it would go on being wafted endlessly and grandly in the air, is a bit of soapy substance on the floor.

Now this is an experience that is not restricted to children. Often that which seemingly has promised so much to our adult hearts has in reality yielded so little.

It was peeping through the brambles, that little wild white rose,
Where the hawthorne hedge was planted, my garden to enclose.
All beyond was fern and heather, on the breezy, open moor;
All within was sun and shelter, and the wealth of beauty's store.
But I did not heed the fragrance of flow'ret or of tree,
For my eyes were on that rosebud, and it grew too high for me.
In vain I strove to reach it through its tangled mass of green,
It only smiled and nodded behind its thorny screen.

. . . .

So in life's wider gardens there are buds of promise, too,
Beyond our reach to gather, but not beyond our view.
                                        —ELLEN H. WILLIS

Have we not yearned for buds in wider gardens to blossom forth? World leaders have promised peace. National politicians have guaranteed security. Endless numbers of remedies have been avowed for scores of problems. But we wake each morning to some new threat of war and millions go to sleep each night cold and hungry. Promises have been made to us so frequently and broken so repeatedly we perhaps have less faith than a child blowing bubbles.

But here is a vow that is valid. Here is a pledge that is

12

true. "Wait for the promise of the Father . . . 'for . . . you shall be baptized with the Holy Spirit.'" It is a promise that has been and will continue to be confirmed —this glorious assurance that the Holy Spirit will come. Jesus had given the disciples his word. He had promised to send the Spirit from the Father and for nineteen hundred years he has been our accessible friend. The baptism of the Spirit, however, as every other blessing, must be a cooperative affair.

What made it possible for this divine pledge to become valid? What enabled the first disciples of Jesus to receive his promised Spirit?

I

First, the disciples believed that the Spirit would come. I am coming more and more to believe that the major reason we are not being something for God and doing something for God lies right at this point. We have failed at that which is most elementary. "If ye shall ask any thing in my name, I will do it." (KJV.) We simply don't believe that. And so we fret with our families, toil monotonously at our tasks, perhaps are faithful though feeble in our worship because we do not really believe that anything we ask will be done. How we need to know that God can do the incredible, even the impossible, for a man, in a man, and with a man if we will only ask him.

These followers of Jesus had faith that what he had promised to do he would do. They had doubted before.

13

After the horror of Calvary they had been completely and utterly defeated. They were not just frustrated men as some have suggested. They were hopeless men. But on the third day the stone was moved—the tomb was empty—their Lord was alive as he promised them he would be. They would not doubt his word again.

How essential it is that we become captives of this truth. The disciples could have faith now for anything the future might hold because their Lord had risen. In a very real sense when he came alive, they came alive. Hope, longing, desire—these were replaced by trust, faith, and certainty. Whatever he had said before, they knew now would surely come to pass.

They remembered the words: "If I do not go away, the Counselor will not come to you; but if I go, I will send him to you." And they believed. Thus knowing the joy of his Resurrection, Christ *with* them, they now believed his promise to send the Spirit, Christ *in* them. They would no longer be men searching for something but men shouting about something. Their one resolve would not be an expedition to find, for they had an experience to tell. They would not be men pursuing truth but proclaiming truth.

Can we not then believe with all our minds that he who came to dwell within them will come to dwell within us? We have a resurrected Savior as supreme evidence that he keeps his word.

When the Gentiles received the Spirit it was a result of Peter's preaching about Christ, climaxed by the words,

"God raised him on the third day." The Spirit will come to our hearts only when we believe Christ came from the tomb.

"Christ is living! Christ is living!" exclaimed R. W. Dale with a burning heart and glowing face. And the English preacher's entire ministry became a sacrament of the Spirit when his heart experienced the living Lord.

II

As the Resurrection gave the disciples faith to believe his Spirit would come, their living Lord also gave them faith to wait until he came. Luke does not tell us that the Holy Spirit came because the disciples busied themselves with labor but because they devoted themselves to prayer. His Holy Presence comes not because we are aggressive but because we are submissive. We may indeed be channels through which the Spirit of Christ strives, strengthens, and blesses. But Mary had learned what her sister, Martha, had failed to realize—the supreme one thing. She had knelt at the Lord's feet before becoming occupied on her own. Thus the disciples learned at Pentecost that he came not as they worked in the vineyard but as they waited for the promise.

The idea of waiting upon the Lord is not merely a New Testament concept. How long Habakkuk had looked for an answer to the age-old problem of why God allows good people to suffer we do not know. But he determined to take his stand on a watchtower and wait for the word of the Lord. The conviction that God's righteousness would some-day fill the earth did not come immediately, just as the leaven does not perform its necessary function at once. But God did disclose that surely his glory would come if the prophet waited.

There is a memorable bit of advice that Samuel gave Saul recorded in the ninth chapter of First Samuel. "Stand thou still a while, that I may shew thee the word of God." (KJV.)

Of course, this is not only true in religion. I imagine Hawthorne was dejected when he lost his position at the custom house in Salem. But it gave him a chance to pro-duce what is in my opinion America's greatest novel, *The Scarlet Letter*. It might never have been written had Haw-thorne not had to stand still awhile.

If it is true that during these still moments we have our greatest thoughts, I think it is also true that we make our highest decisions. The Master could go through the ordeal of Calvary because of the brave obedience of Geth-semane.

But you may ask, though the disciples waited, is the same thing required of us? It would be well for us to re-member that we do not receive the Holy Spirit on our terms but on his.

Most assuredly I would not declare a time limit on spirit baptism. It is certainly true that we receive all of his Spirit we are capable of receiving when we are converted. But these gates of new life do not open fully until we possess the stillness of mind and hunger of heart that are essential.

No matter how emotional one's encounter with Christ, such encounter need never be irrational. Did not Isaiah hear God woo Israel with this invitation, "Come now, let us reason together"? And Paul counted commitment to Christ a "worship offered by *mind* and heart" (Rom. 12:1 NEB).

What transformed the man of Tarsus from persecutor to preacher? The question as Saul called from the Damascus road was: "Who are you?" And the answer was: "I am Jesus." In that moment of realization and surrender, Saul was becoming Paul.

In like manner he received the Holy Spirit. Three days in Damascus—three days of holy hush alone with God in the house of Judas—this preceded the Spirit's entrance into his life.

> How silently, how silently
>   The wondrous gift is given!
> So God imparts to human hearts
>   The blessings of His heaven.
> No ear may hear His coming,
>   But in this world of sin,
> Where meek souls will receive Him still,
>   The dear Christ enters in.
>   —PHILLIPS BROOKS

With the saving gospel in his heart and on his lips, Paul journeyed from the Damascus road across the Roman world. But his becoming actively aggressive was entirely

17

dependent upon his being deeply committed and completely certain.

III

The disciples believed the Spirit would come. Gripped by this faith, they waited for him. Then with the power of that Presence, they began the witness that led through Jerusalem, Judea, Samaria, and to the ends of the earth. "With great power," says Luke, "the apostles gave their testimony.

Follow them as they go out, these Spirit-filled men of the daring young church. And whether you journey with Philip to Gaza, Peter to Joppa, Paul to Jerusalem, or Barnabas to Antioch, you find men so possessed by a passion that our own hearts are kindled by that flame.

It is a continuing glory, thank God! The book of Acts has not been completed. There are yet mission posts that have not been reached. There are yet souls that have not been touched. Not only Macedonians but world citizens everywhere are calling. Through his Spirit we are adequate to answer.

"Two things amaze me," said a young nurse on a college campus. "The first is that he loved me enough to save me, and the second is that he trusts me enough to use me."

And he will use us. Wherever there is a cold hearth, a bare table, an ignorant mind, a diseased body, a wasted life—the Macedonian cry still comes. When we hear the cry to come and help, the Spirit bids us to go and minister.

Many people thought David Livingstone was lost. Of course, as S. D. Gordon pointed out, the truth was he was not lost in Africa. He was only lost in utter devotion to the needy who cried, "Come and help." Not knowing that he stayed in Africa by choice, the editor of the *New York Herald* sent for one of his reporters, Henry Stanley. "Find Livingstone," said James G. Bennett to Stanley. "How much money do you place at my disposal?" asked Stanley. "Fifty thousand dollars, or a larger sum. Never mind about the money," said Bennett, "find Livingstone."

Now God has children who are lost. Many are lost because they have never glimpsed enough light to realize they are in the dark. But many others are lost by their own choice not in selfless dedication, like Livingstone, but in selfish existence.

For the sake of these wandering ones, God commissions us to find them and bring them back to him. All the treasures of his infinite grace wait for our employment in the quest. But better than all his mercies, he has promised to go with us himself in the strength of the Spirit. The decision to serve is ours! The moment to start is now!

II
THE
ASCENSION

As they were looking on, he was lifted up, and a cloud took him out of their sight.
—ACTS 1:9

"Paint Christ not dead but risen," said Michelangelo. "Paint him the conqueror of death! The Lord of life!"

The Gospel artists may have had differences in their several accounts of the ministry of Jesus. But there is complete agreement in each of their narratives as to the dynamic climax. It is this: Christ is not dead but risen. He is the conqueror of death! He is the Lord of life!

Matthew and Mark, for instance, paint him as the Lord who commissions. That is, he is pictured as the Supreme Commander who assigns his followers the task of claiming the world in his name.

The pinnacle of Luke's Gospel is reached with the telling of the beautiful Emmaus story. And, of course, it is designed to create that inner assurance on which all purposeful outward activity must be based. Cleopas and his friend said of the Companion who had journeyed with them: "Did we not feel our hearts on fire as he talked with us on the road and explained the scriptures to us?" (Luke 24:32 NEB).

Perhaps the most significant appearance of our Lord in the Gospel of John is that scene on the Galilean beach. Here the Master asked Simon if he loved him. He did not ask Peter if he loved sheep. Nor did he ask him if he loved to tend sheep. "Do you love me?" That was the paramount question. Loving people and loving to help them is possible only when we love Christ.

So we may think of Jesus as the Lord of the outward task or the inward flame or the loving heart. But regardless, the evangelists would have us know he is our eternally living Savior. This brings us to the purpose of his departure back to the Father. We wonder perhaps after his victory over death why he felt it imperative to go away. What a marvelous time, we may feel, to have made visible the Kingdom. Did not the disciples who had been so weak need his physical ministration in building that Kingdom?

He had commissioned them to make disciples of all nations. Would they not need his physical guidance to discharge such a task? He had disappeared after having caused their hearts to burn. Would they not need his reappearing presence to keep the flame aglow? He had asked Peter if he loved him. Would not Simon need his appearance if he were to share his affection?

Yet he said, "It is for your good that I am leaving you." (John 16:7 NEB.) How could this be possible? What is the actual meaning of the ascension? Why did Christ go away?

I

In the first place, Christ's departure enabled him to show us the ministry of intercession.

We are aware of the Master's prayer life during his physical ministry. We read in one place, "He went into the hills to pray." And again, "As he was praying, the appearance of his countenance was altered." No wonder one of his disciples urged him to teach them to pray the way he prayed. No doubt these disciples had said prayers most of their lives. But they noticed the power that it gave to their Lord. For him prayer was far more than routine ritual. Mere synagogue ceremony had never made their faith real and their faces radiant. They knew that whatever was taking place on those mountain pilgrimages they needed. Hence the request, "Teach us to pray."

We also are conscious of the fact that our Lord stressed

intercession as a very definite part of prayer. In the Upper Room, Jesus told Simon that though Satan desired him, he had been praying for him that his faith might not fail! That is, he had been pleading to the Father in his behalf for stout-hearted commitment. Again in the garden we hear his earnest appeal, "I pray for them; . . . because they belong to thee" (John 17:9 NEB). Thus it must be that he who intervened so intensely for them would not break faith when he was taken from them. Paul told the church at Rome that Christ at God's right hand pleads our cause.

But you may be asking what is the purpose of intercessory prayer. Mark says that when the disciples went forth to preach, the Lord worked with them and confirmed the message. How did he work with them? Certainly by the demonstration of the power of the Spirit. But since he had already ascended, we realize that he also worked with them by interceding for them.

Of course, we should not attempt to classify the work of the Savior and the Spirit in too fine a fashion. Jesus, for instance, referred to the Holy Spirit as an advocate and we realize that word advocate means intercessor. Too, we find Paul saying that since "we do not know how to pray worthily as sons of God, . . . his Spirit within us is actually praying for us" (Rom. 8:26 Phillips).

The author of Hebrews says that Jesus "is always living to intercede" (Heb. 7:25 Phillips).

> In the hour of trial,
> Jesus, plead for me;

Lest by base denial,
  I depart from Thee.
When Thou seest me waver,
  with a look recall,
Nor for fear or favor
  Suffer me to fall.
    —JAMES MONTGOMERY

If our Lord is an example of intercession, he is also an exhorter for intercession. In speaking to his disciples Jesus told them to pray for those who might abuse them. When Paul was giving his first fatherly counsel to young Timothy, he also advised that prayer be offered for all men.

I shall never forget going to a distant state to preach at a Sunday morning service. The Holy Spirit moved upon us with great power. People were converted. Lives were changed. Church members who had grown cold walked in the glory of a new experience. What had started out to be a single meeting became a mighty week of revival.

One afternoon the pastor took me to see an elderly blind woman. She was a winsome Christian and humbly confided that she had prayed for years for such an outpouring of the Spirit upon the community she loved. After we had gone, her minister said to me that he felt her prayers had caused this amazing season of blessedness.

II

Then, the Ascension teaches us that we need not merely place our faith in things visible.

To be sure one may feel at times more certain when he can see that to which his hope clings. I am in sympathy with the little boy who was awakened one night by the sound of thunder. Hurriedly he ran into his parents' bedroom and told them he was scared. "The storm cannot harm you," said his mother. "Besides, the Lord is in the room with you." "I know," he answered, "but I want somebody in there with skin on him."

There are times when we all share that feeling. We have known those moments of need when we longed for the face of a friend and the grip of a hand. When that trusted person came our way, he brought with him such gaiety of spirit and courage of heart that somehow the lights were turned on in our souls again. We then were able to face the future with a renewed confidence.

The Baptizer came to that particular place. Tired, lonely, and discouraged he sent a pathetic inquiry from his prison cell to Jesus: "Are you the one?" That is, John was asking, "Is what I have been preaching true? Across Judea I have been proclaiming that the kingdom of heaven is at hand. I have been telling that the Lamb of God is here. Is it really so? Are you the Savior who is to redeem the world?"

John knew better than that. He recognized the Christ when first he saw him and said so. He was anything but a faithless man. It was his faithful and forceful preaching that cost him his freedom and later his life. Why did he linger briefly in the doorway of doubt? Because in a dungeon's depression he longed for more than a memory. He yearned to touch again the hand he had held at Jordan.

Our Lord knew what it meant to feel forsaken. How he needed the courage of companionship that night in Gethsemane. "Stay awake with me," he said to his disciples. "My heart is ready to break with grief." (Matt. 26:38 NEB.)

Jesus came as a physical presence to prepare us for the spiritual life. He was visibly seen that he could be invisibly known. When we understand this, we can see the reason why he forbade Mary to embrace him in the Garden. Holding him always, knowing him forever is not a physical experience. He told her to go and say to the disciples: "I am ascending." This then was the fellowship that they were to know and we are to share—the unseen but everpresent companionship of the Spirit.

Thus he was teaching them as he teaches us that he does not have to be seen to be known. It is enough if we "believe that he exists and that he rewards those who search for him" (Heb. 11:6 NEB). Recall once more his message to Thomas who had doubted even the witness of his brethren: "Happy are they who never saw me and yet have found faith" (John 20:29 NEB).

III

This brings us to the last point which has already been anticipated. What is the meaning of the ascension? Here is the point of supreme significance: Had he not gone, he could not have come. He said to his disciples that if he did not depart, the Helper (Moffatt's word for Spirit) would not come.

Read again those bewildering words in the Upper Room: "It is for your good that I am leaving you." How could it be for their good? Once while he was away from them a father brought his epileptic boy to them to be healed but they could not do it. How could his departure be to their advantage when his absence so weakened their faith? And he continues: "If I go, I will send him [the Helper] to you." (Moffatt.) And again, "He remains with you and will be within you." (John 14:17 Moffatt.)

No longer were they to depend on outward association. They would have inner assurance. Everything in his ministry pointed to this. In a very real sense the Master's entire life had been a prelude to spiritual baptism. The goal of the incarnate Christ is the indwelling Spirit.

Thus when he dwells within, he is no longer confined to one place. He is able to be everywhere. He was no longer simply present at Bethany or Jericho or in an upper room. He was with his disciples because he was in his disciples wherever they were. Consequently Mark tells us that the Lord confirmed the Word as they preached it everywhere. Then he is no longer limited to a single group. He is capable of being with everyone. He was no longer on the road with just twelve or in Matthew's house with a crowd or even on a mountain with a vast company.

After Stephen had been stoned, the young church was severely oppressed. As a result the disciples were scattered.

Wherever they were dispersed, however, because of the Holy Presence abiding in their hearts, they preached.

Some months ago I sought to win a man for Christ. When the claims of the Savior had been rejected, I must admit I left his home rather sadly. But a few days later he stood up publicly and declared his faith in Christ. When we were alone he said, "After you left, the Lord continued to speak to me. In the quiet of my bedroom, I knelt and gave him my life." The Lord continued to speak! I believe he was with me in the next home I visited that day. But he never left the first home. He remained until he was received.

Finally, he is longer restricted to one period. He is accessible at all times. He is not merely on a beach with a man possessed by demons or by a well with a woman who was an outcast or at a cave wherein one lay dead that he had loved. He is the ever-available Presence. "I am with you always," he says.

Here is a man whose life has been exceedingly difficult. Failing vision has forced him to be entirely dependent on the eyesight of others. While young he had been disappointed by one who found his partial blindness too great a burden to share. He has reached middle age now. He is alone one night in his manse passing through a period of great despair. Perhaps unhappy memories have caused him to be depressed. Possibly doubts have invaded the sanctuary of his soul. Whatever the cause for his despondency, we know he is suffering much mental pain. Suddenly he turns to him who has promised never to forsake. Although he has been a Christian for years, in the strength of this friendship he finds fresh inspiration and new hope. And he wrote about it. Here is the lovely poem, the fruit of his faith:

> O Love that wilt not let me go,
>   I rest my weary soul in Thee;
> I give Thee back the life I owe,
> That in Thine ocean depths its flow
>   May richer, fuller be.
>   —GEORGE MATHESON

This assurance can be yours. "I will not leave you forlorn; I am coming to you." (John 14:18 Moffatt.) He did and he will.

III
THE EXPERIENCE
OF PENTECOST

When the day of Pentecost had come, they were all together in one place . . . . And they were all filled with the Holy Spirit.   —ACTS 2:1, 4

This was the day Christ had promised. Beginning with Easter Day, Jesus had appeared at different intervals to the apostles. They knew now beyond the shadow of any doubt he was their eternally living Lord. Then after his ascension, they had waited in prayerful expectation for the divine pledge to be fulfilled. "All these with one accord devoted themselves to prayer." (Acts 1:14.)

Perhaps they did not as yet understand how his assurance would be disclosed. We realize this as we hear the question put to him, "Lord, will you at this time restore the kingdom to Israel?" Doubtless most of them, if not all of them, were still expecting a king to appear and build an earthly empire. But he did not return visibly to conquer the world with force. He came back invisibly to redeem the world with love. "Before many days," he had promised them on Mount Olivet, "you shall be baptized with the Holy Spirit."

Now the disciples were familiar with the word "spirit." They had heard the story of creation and that the Spirit of God moved upon the face of the waters. They had read tales of their heroes: Samson, David, Ezekiel, and others upon whom the Spirit of God had moved mightily. They understood spirit to mean the outward manifestation of God's power; however, spirit means also the inward revelation of God's presence. This they had yet to learn.

Pentecost was the day of enlightenment. Thus empowered, the disciples began love's conquest of the world.

Now Pentecost is not an isolated event. It is what God always wants to do for his church and his children. The Holy Spirit meant new life, great power, constant concern to his disciples. It means exactly that for us today.

It has already been suggested how those first followers experienced Pentecost. How may we experience it?

I

First, we must *repent*. When Peter had finished preaching his Pentecost sermon, the people asked, "What shall we do?" His initial answer was, "Repent."

Now some will say that this is the primary requirement of conversion. Did not our Lord make this basic for entrance into the Kingdom? Not only did he lay stress upon repentance when he first preached in Galilee but the last time he was with his disciples he declared that they must preach it, too. "Repentance bringing the forgiveness of sins is to be proclaimed to all nations," he had said. (Luke 24: 47 NEB.)

But if it is essential for conversion, repentance is just as necessary for consecration. If one is sincere, he must admit that the more he seeks the Father's presence, the more he sees his soul's unworthiness. The Lord on the throne put Isaiah on his knees. In all probability he had always been a believer. But in the Temple he became a repenter. And it opened the door to his becoming the prophetic power of Jerusalem. Make no mistake about it. The Lord cannot remake us into what we should be unless there is a sense of regret over what we have been.

I speak now not of false humility that may express itself in public sorrow. I am speaking of the quiet awareness in the secret place of the Most High that we have sinned and fallen short of his glory. Closeness depends on confession— not to the world but to him.

"I die every day," said Paul. He confronted death daily, and the power to face the whips, mobs, and beasts came as a result of being continually repentant, forgiven, and blessed. But we can never know daily forgiveness and blessing until there is daily sorrow for sin. Pentecost only comes as we are constantly penitent in his presence.

Then, we must *request*. Desire is always the prelude to dedication. The Spirit never comes until the heart yearns for him. When in humility we beseech the Divine Presence to home within our hearts, he enters. And only our willful rejection of him can ever break the tie that binds.

> The soul that on Jesus still leans for repose,
> I will not, I will not desert to his foes.

But the leaning heart is first the longing heart. We must ask before we can own. Here are the words of our Lord: "If you, then bad as you are, know how to give your children what is good for them, how much more will the heavenly Father give the Holy Spirit to those who ask him!" (Luke 11:13 NEB.)

> I got up early one morning
> And rushed right into the day;
> I had so much to accomplish
> That I didn't take time to pray.
> Problems just tumbled about me,
> And heavier became each task.
> "Why doesn't God help me?" I wondered.
> He answered, "You didn't ask."

I wanted to see joy and beauty
But the day toiled on, grey and bleak.
I wondered why God didn't show me,
He said, "But you didn't seek."
I tried to come into God's presence;
I used all my keys at the lock,
God gently and lovingly chided,
"My child, you didn't knock."
I woke up early this morning
And paused before entering the day.
I had so much to accomplish
That I had to take time to pray.[1]

How many of us are spiritually unable to meet life's problems because we have not asked for Christ's presence. Our Lord himself felt this desire must not be simply a lukewarm wish but a wholehearted need. "Blessed are those who hunger and thirst for righteousness," he said, "for they shall be satisfied." (Matt. 5:6.)

Then if we are to experience Pentecost, we must surely *receive* it. "You shall receive the gift of the Spirit," said Peter. Now it is so very important that we understand this particular point. Often we miss conversion and commitment right here.

How are we saved? Not by doing something but by accepting something. "God so loved that he gave." Salvation is a gift. If the lost man would be found he must accept the gift. If the backslider would be reinstated, he must accept the gift.

[1] Louise Dawson, "Time to Pray," *Power* (October-November-December, 1949). Used by permission.

Four years after Milton wrote *Paradise Lost,* he wrote the sequel, *Paradise Regained.* But deliverance from sin is never regained. It is always regiven.

How are we to become consecrated? Not by accomplishing but by accepting. Now there comes a time when it is absurd even to ask. Would not the disciples have appeared foolish in the Upper Room begging for the loaf and the cup—when their Master was saying, "Take; this is my body." "This is my blood." Even so when the heart is repentant and when in humility we request his presence to enter our lives, he will surely come.

If we are to keep the experience of Pentecost, we must *reveal* the Spirit to others. The Lord commanded the disciples to do this. "You will receive power when the Holy Spirit comes upon you," he had said, "and you will bear witness for me." (Acts 1:8 NEB.) I am not sure but that this is our only real purpose for living. If Christ came to reveal God then we are converted and consecrated to reveal Christ.

Do you remember when Peter and John were arrested in Jerusalem? They had healed a cripple so they were brought to court and interrogated on the witness stand.

"In whose name have you done this thing?" the council questioned. "In the name of Christ," they answered. As a result of such holy boldness, Luke says that the Jewish rulers recognized them as men who had been with Jesus. The words "had been" are true, but the words "were with" could likewise be inserted. Even on the witness stand, we are told that Peter was filled with the Spirit.

Thus in prison or out—wherever they were—they were revealers of his presence. I know of nothing so marvelous as this: He uses us to make himself known to others.

Years ago I was preaching a revival meeting in a small country church. There was a young chap about twelve years old who was my close friend all week. I remember that he walked with me to my car the night the last service had concluded. "Mr. Chappell," he said slowly, "this week has meant everything to me." Then, without any attempt to be emotional or dramatic, he added, "Because of you I have seen Christ."

Long since I have spent the monetary gift those kindly hill-folk gave me. But I have kept the lad's words in the treasure house of my heart. I get them out every now and then to look at them and to humbly thank God for them and most of all to beg him to make them constantly true.

II

Thus experiencing Pentecost, what does the entrance of the Holy Spirit mean in our lives today?

The most important meaning is this: We have his *unfailing presence*. Our Lord promised that the Holy Spirit would be the disciples' constant Companion. He had told them they would not be left forlorn. When the Master speaks of the gift of his presence, he also uses the word "forever." But not only did Jesus assure them of his abiding nearness, he made them aware that his availability meant more than just companionship. He was to be their unquestionable leader. Jesus said of the Holy Spirit: "He will teach you all things." Also, "He will guide you into all the truth."

How little the Master said about the specific evils of his day. Except for scathing denunciations of religious pretense, he named few sins. But he was always asking people to come to him and to follow him and to trust him.

So today! Where do we get the idea that war is wrong and that all men should live in peace? How can we know where to stand in regard to the crucial race issues which confront us? What standard is lifted to guide us as we proclaim purity for personality and salvation for society?

To be sure some of the things Christ said steer us in the direction we must take. But above all—he will teach, he will guide. Our Quaker friends refer to this as Inner Light. It is his Presence that points the path.

Thus admitting his unfailing presence we have *unceasing power*. The different New Testament translators have varied names for the Holy Spirit. He is called the Comforter, the Counselor, our Advocate, and the Divine Helper. But one word is invariably used when these writers describe what the Holy Spirit will do for Christ's followers. "You shall receive *power*," said Jesus.

Now certainly this was true for those with whom our Savior lived. There was as much difference in the disciples before and after Pentecost as there is in midnight and midday. "The disciples *all* deserted him and ran away." (Mark 14:50 NEB.) But let the Spirit be received and then look. "With great power the apostles gave their testimony . . . and great grace was upon them *all*." These were

37

changed men. They were no longer power-less. They were power-filled. There was just one reason: His Spirit had come.

I am thinking of two ministers who are devoted friends. During their seminary days they often visited together and occasionally preached for each other. On a certain evening one of the young men took his mother to hear his friend preach. Though profiting by the sermon she was a bit surprised at the force of the message. "Your friend has an inborn talent," she said to her son. "No, mother," he answered, "he has an indwelling Spirit."

We do not need another Pentecost. There is nothing wrong with the one we have. His Spirit which made dynamic disciples in Jerusalem is available now if we are willing to be receivers of that power.

Finally, receiving his Spirit means that we shall have an *unyielding passion* for the souls of men. After Pentecost you do not find the disciples forsaking or fleeing or following at a distance. They are men whose supreme intent is to tell what a risen Christ can do for a believing heart.

When ordered not to speak his name in public, they answered, "We cannot give up speaking of what we have seen and heard." (Acts 4:20 Moffatt.) And when the Sanhedrin had them flogged, they rejoiced that they had been considered worthy to suffer dishonor for Christ. Instead of such entreaties and beatings silencing them or scaring them, Luke tells us that not for a single day did they cease to teach and preach the gospel of Jesus.

They were to find that this gospel was not restricted.

Because of their consecrated concern, the Gentiles, Israel's lost sheep, would be included. It was a great day of enlightenment for Simon Peter when the Spirit broke the bonds of prejudice that had bound him. He could now say, "God has no favourites, but that in every nation the man who is god-fearing and does what is right is acceptable to him." (Acts 10:34-35 NEB.)

And so the witness continued until we know the truth of Joel's prophecy which was really the text for Simon's sermon at Pentecost: "All who call upon the name of the Lord shall be delivered" (Joel 2:32).

Had these disciples sought to keep Pentecost for themselves they would have lost both its meaning for their own lives and its message for the world. The Spirit-filled life must always result in the Spirit-shared life.

"What makes you think your friend is convinced of the presence of God," one layman asked another. "Because he convinces me," was the reply.

Are we the channels for his saving grace that we ought to be? Or could it be that we have neglected to go and tell because we have not knelt and received? We do not obey his summons for we have not admitted his spirit.

Pentecost is now. His presence is real. The Holy Spirit is here. And he is yours if you want him!

IV
DOORWAYS
TO DEDICATION

They continued steadily learning the teaching of the apostles, and joined in their fellowship, in the breaking of bread, and in prayer. —ACTS 2:42 *Phillips*

What a day Pentecost had been! Not only had Jerusalem felt a new power, it had seen new men.

Now sincere men must not only interest themselves in being saved, they must be concerned about staying saved. Religious education is not some modern contrivance instituted for this purpose. There was never a better program for Christian nurture than that inaugurated after Pentecost.

Three thousand people had been converted. How were they to stay faithful? How were they to grow stronger? These first disciples who had walked with the Lord during his earthly ministry thought of themselves as keepers of the flame. Guided by the Holy Spirit, what plan for spiritual edification was put forth by these sentinels of the Spirit?

I

First, they instructed the new disciples in their apostolic teaching. Actually it was not so much their teaching as it was what they had been taught by Jesus.

Now we do not know precisely point by point what the apostles taught these new converts. But we can be sure of two things that were continually stressed.

The first was that Jesus was Savior. "The Son of man came to seek and to save the lost," Jesus had said. "Whoever calls on the name of the Lord shall be saved." This was the theme of Pentecost, and from Pentecost on it was to be proclaimed with power by the good news witnesses. They constantly preached Christ. His name means anointed. Anointed for what? To save. The converted life was their first emphasis.

J. B. Phillips has a paragraph in his preface to the translation of Acts that is pertinent. He writes: "The call of the Good News was not the emphasis on man's sinfulness, but that the Man Jesus Whom many of them had known personally was no less than God's chosen One. . . . The

41

Good News was that if men would turn from their former ways and accept the forgiveness of God through Christ, then the Spirit of God was living and available to enter their hearts and transform them."

Thus teaching the Pentecost converts that Jesus was Savior, these new disciples themselves became evangelists, preaching this message of transformation. And always the Holy Spirit gave them faith and power as they testified. The truth that redeemed them is what we must exhort today. The Divine Helper still gives the strength to deliver it.

Our one hope for this world is not wealthy men, nor even brilliant men, but twice-born men. Preaching Christ to the lost is not the only business of the church, but it is the supreme business of the church. If we fail here, it matters little how we succeed on the outskirts. The central truth is always the saving truth.

The second thing continually stressed was that Jesus was Lord. "You call me 'Master' and 'Lord,' and rightly so," said Jesus. (John 13:13 NEB.) "Let all Israel then accept as certain that God has made this Jesus . . . both Lord and Messiah," said Peter at Pentecost. (Acts 2:36 NEB.)

He was not only their deliverer; he was their master— the dominant Ruler of their lives. If the converted life was their first emphasis, the controlled life followed closely. They were men who acted upon the orders of a supreme commander—the Holy Spirit.

If you say this smacks of dogmatism and sounds dictatorial, then I must answer, You are right. Let me hasten further to point out that our Lord never extended easy invitations to the Christ-life. He never told a man to come in the Kingdom without counting the cost. He never invited a man to share in a fellowship that offered cushions for sitting and crutches for standing.

He did say, "If anyone comes to me and does not hate his father and mother, wife and children, brothers and sisters, even his own life, he cannot be a disciple of mine." (Luke 14:26 NEB.) Does that sound like we are being summoned to a pink-tea social?

Here again are the words of the preacher at Pentecost: "Repent therefore, and turn again, that your sins may be blotted out." Do these indicate that all one must do is choose the church that is friendly and the sanctuary that is air-conditioned and the minister who is not meddlesome?

The fact is Jesus only promised two things: a Cross to bear and a Companion to bless. These men of the young church were acquainted with both. They had yielded themselves fully. Christ was Lord of their lives.

II

The new followers of the Way joined in the dedicated fellowship. For a while the group was merely a Jewish society, but it was destined to become a society of all believers.

How it must have strengthened these immature disciples to be joined in hand and heart with men who had personally known Jesus. This was the first part of the fellowship—companions of commitment.

43

What was the difference between their fellowship and ours? The main contrast lay in purpose. Think of the things we sometimes say to people today in attempting to persuade them to attend our churches. "The service just lasts an hour." "You will meet people who may be beneficial to you since you are new in the community." "We only have one service a week, therefore church obligations will not stifle your leisure time." "We have the nicest cushioned pews."

But these men upon whom the Spirit had fallen in such mighty power met for only two reasons. First, they yearned to get closer to God. They had been told by their Lord that if they as earthly parents knew how to give gifts to their children, how much more the heavenly Father desired to give the Holy Spirit to them if they wished him. And they deeply longed for him not to be their occasional inspiration but their abiding Friend.

A religious renaissance seems to be taking place in many parts of our nation today. There are indications that some of these revivals are genuine and that much lasting good is being accomplished. But we are not always able to measure spiritual vitality by church attendance. The church where Jesus first preached in Nazareth no doubt was crowded, but that crowd wanted to kill him when he finished his sermon.

The hope of our world is not churches filled with people but people who are filled with Christ!

Then these disciples longed to grow closer to one another. Luke tells us things like these: "All who believed were together and had all things in common"; "Now the com-

44

pany of those who believed were of one heart and soul."

It is distressing to observe people quarreling over trifles. I am not speaking of simple differences, for all of us on occasions disagree. Yet I have never seen church people disagree when considering whether they were going to devote one night or two nights a week to seeking out the unsaved. I have never seen church members fall out when discussing whether it would be better to sponsor one mission church or two. And I do not recall ever attending a meeting where there was serious conflict as to how many days of special prayer should be set aside during Lent for the edification of the church.

But I have seen individuals fairly fly into a rage where a few dollars were at stake. I have seen officials go home after an evening session not speaking to one another because of opposing opinions on the selection of a chairman of a minor committee.

I was preaching in a church some years ago and everyone seemed out of sorts. I finally found out why and I was shocked at the littleness of it. Some felt the lace on the sacrament table was too long. Others argued that it was too short. You can readily understand why this church was not a force for righteousness in that area. May God have mercy on our selfish smallness and help us to be as one as we go on our pilgrimage.

But if these disciples were companions of commitment, they were also companions of commission. Their task was more than one of taking in. They were men who were reaching out. Fresh from receiving, they were now delivering the good tidings of great joy: Jesus saves. And when we read in Acts that they spoke the word of God with boldness and that "with great power the apostles gave their testimony," we see clearly the stress placed upon witness.

I well remember attending a dinner party one night while I was in seminary. Those present were preachers and teachers who were unusually close friends. Somehow the topic of conversation got around to other vocations we might have chosen had we not answered the call to some phase of the Christian ministry. One friend, who was a teacher, said that if he were not teaching theology he would probably be a professor in the field of English literature. The next man said that if he were not preaching in all probability he would be selling insurance. Another suggested that if he were not a minister he would very likely be coaching in some athletic capacity. One of the group who spoke was a young man whose life and witness had meant much on our campus. At one time he had lived a dissipated life, but the Lord had wonderfully changed him. "My friends," he said with unashamed tears in his eyes, "I have never thought of doing anything else but telling people about Christ, since I responded to him myself." This young man voiced the principal assignment of the early church and a determining factor in why it was so powerful.

III

The new converts, along with those who had known Jesus personally, broke bread together.

Paul was the first to use the expression, "Lord's supper." Nevertheless, the original disciples probably celebrated this event many times before Paul's conversion.

The intimacy of that evening experience in the Upper Room had not been forgotten. The Master had not intended that it should. Knowing that Calvary was very near, Jesus felt it essential that the disciples encounter some radiant reality they would always remember. As he realized the ordeal through which he was to pass, he likewise knew the Gethsemanes and Golgothas that waited for them. There would be times of suffering. There would be days of anguish. But the memory of those mountain moments would be recalled. And somehow the crosses would not seem as heavy and the prison cells would not seem as lonely when they remembered they belonged to the Royal Order of the Redeemed.

Thus, as we consider the phrase, "the breaking of bread," we can be certain the disciples taught the new followers what they had learned from Jesus in the Upper Room.[1] To become a participant in this communion meant to be wholeheartedly involved in Calvary discipleship: "As you eat this bread and drink the cup, you proclaim the Lord's death" (I Cor. 11:26).

But the "breaking of bread" means something else which is of consequence. In truth every meal was to be a sacrament. We sometimes refer to the Lord's supper as the

---

[1] Paul's knowledge of what happened in the Upper Room as he relates it in I Cor. 11:23-26 could only have come from the fact that he himself was taught by traditional instruction.

Eucharist. This comes from the Greek word *eucharistia* which means the giving of thanks. If we could understand and practice this, every meal time would be a hallowed hour. Often the "blessing" or grace requested at the table is so conventional. We pray a routine prayer and then participate in conversation our Lord would be embarrassed to hear. But when bread is broken for his sake and in his name and with his presence, the fellowship is a joy and every supper becomes sacred.

One of the loveliest of all Gospel stories is the one where Jesus journeyed with the two disciples to Emmaus. Of course, the reason he joined them was so they might realize him in risen certainty. But do you recall when it was that they recognized him? Not when he first drew near to them. Not when they told him the things they had been discussing. Nor was it even when he spoke to them from the Scriptures. But when they sat down to eat, he took the bread, blessed it, brake it, and gave it to them. I prefer Phillips translation here: "Their eyes opened wide and they knew him!" No wonder the veteran disciples thought such an experience was worth sharing with these fresh recruits.

IV

Finally, these new followers became disciples of prayer. One of the twelve had once asked the Lord to teach them how to pray. Now they became instructors as they guided these new men of the way along the highest road of consecration. There are many paths to his presence, but the

48

prayer-way is the soul's grandest avenue to blessedness and usefulness.

Probably the disciples taught the value of praying in the Temple. That was the reason Peter and John were going there when they healed the lame man at its gate. Jesus had felt that prayer was the main reason one should go to the Temple. That was why he had been so angry when he found that it had been desecrated into a market-place for trade. "My house shall be a house of prayer"; he said, "but you have made it a robbers' cave." (Luke 19:46 NEB.)

But it was most likely in the homes that prayer was given supreme attention. Paul uses the phrase "the church in your house." We have every right to believe that it continued to be an Upper Room experience not only in the home of John Mark's mother but indeed throughout this new community of the consecrated. We read that "day after day in the Temple and in people's houses they continued to teach unceasingly and to proclaim the Good News of Jesus Christ" (Acts 5:42 Phillips). It is difficult to believe they would have neglected that which made their teaching possible and their preaching powerful.

We know that on one occasion Peter and John were charged not to speak the name of Jesus. After being released they went back to their own company and held a prayer meeting. What was the result of it? "When they had prayed, the place in which they were gathered together was shaken; and they were all filled with the Holy Spirit." (Acts 4:31.)

Then the threats meant nothing for they continued to preach Christ with courage and conviction.

Now, I doubt if these disciples could have explained scientifically the component parts of prayer. They might not have been able to explain to modern satisfaction how conviction grew and courage came. But there was one thing they could tell. They knew the indwelling Christ was their priceless possession and the way to keep him was to bear witness. This is what we are lacking today. Prayer is not a test-tube axiom to be proved but a heartfelt certainty to be lived. It is not so much what we can prove but him whom we know that matters.

"Do you know your husband's theory of relativity?" someone asked Mrs. Einstein. "I know very little about my husband's theories," she answered, "but I know my husband." I am persuaded the only real reason we should pray is for an ever deeper knowledge of Christ.

Apostolic instruction—fellowship—breaking bread—prayer. Those who dared follow Christ walked through these doorways guided by the Holy Spirit and changed their world.

The world in which we live today also needs to be changed. Through these doors we now may walk. His Presence still will lead. Are you ready to enter?

V
SOMEONE MUST WAIT ON THE TABLES

The Twelve called the whole body of disciples together and said, "It would be a grave mistake for us to neglect the word of God in order to wait at table." —ACTS 6:2 NEB

This text introduces us to an incident that occurred during the early days of the New Testament church which I think demands our careful examination. There was the feeling that certain people were being neglected in the daily food distribution. Therefore a handful of men were chosen to attend to this prosaic responsibility.

There is no such thing as an inferior task in the King's service. Every commission is sacred, every assignment is notable in the eyes of our Lord if the deed be done for his sake.

As there is no unimportant mission, so there is no unimportant person who toils for the Kingdom. True, some duties are more sensational, some disciples more in the limelight than others. I was just a child when I heard Gypsy Smith, but I can still remember the force with which he spoke, the pathos in his voice. Though I am inspired by the consecration of Billy Graham, I am impressed at the same time with his physical appearance, for he is a handsome man and has a striking personality.

One cold night, years ago, in Yokohama I heard Toyohiko Kagawa. His voice lacked force. Should you have passed him on the street not knowing who he was, you would not have looked twice. But this little tubercular patient was so filled with the Spirit of God that it would be impossible to travel many back streets of the Japanese cities before you would meet saved souls and lifted lives because of his influence.

I must confess here that the most blessed witnesses I have known and the greatest soul winners I have seen have not been the people who made the greatest outward impression but those who have had the deepest inward devotion.

The church today does not need skill so much as it needs surrender. The hope of evangelism is not how capable you are but how committed you are. Let us get away from the idea of great and little persons, promoted and demoted stations, successful and fruitless endeavors. Instead let us ask: Are we yielded to Christ; is our vocation a sacrament; are we giving our witness?

Keeping this in mind let us now look directly at the incident from which our text comes and seek the guidance of the Holy Spirit as we anticipate its meaning for our lives.

I

The Hellenists were complaining because they felt their widows were being overlooked in the food allotment. Luke tells us that there was not a needy person among the company of believers. Now, although we have elsewhere references to property and possessions, this must allude to a common food stock out of which each was receiving a fair amount.

These Hellenists or Greeks were no doubt Jews. But they are distinguished from the Hebrews in the fact that they were not native Jews. They were visitors to Jerusalem who had become captives of the Holy Spirit and had allied themselves with the other followers of Christ. It is possible that the "Hebrews" looked down upon their sojourning cousins and did not completely include them in the necessary supply of rations. This, however, is doubtful. If they did not belong to Jewish lineage by race they belonged by choice. If they were not the same in family, they were the same in faith and this is the only true measurement for orthodoxy.

I think rather that if these Greek widows were being overlooked it was neither because of prejudice nor even of carelessness but because there were no specific persons instructed in such an undertaking. Everyone's task becomes no one's task, hence the necessity for organization.

One other point should be made before we pass on. Seven men were appointed to the duty of distributing food. But it was because of the genuine concern, the sincere compassion of the followers of Christ, that made this care for their bodies possible.

In a meeting I was attending recently two men were discussing our failure to reach the destitute—those who had both physical wants and spiritual needs. "We don't have the know-how," the first suggested. "We don't have the care-how," the other replied. I suppose both are true. But is not the second man more nearly correct? These disciples made provisions for feeding the people because they cared.

Jesus related a parable concerning one who was traveling from Jerusalem to Jericho. He was attacked by robbers who gave him a brutal beating and left him by the roadside to die. Along that same road a priest passed and later a Levite. There can be only one reason why they did not help the wounded man. They did not care. Jesus said they passed by on the other side when they saw him. How terrible a thing it is to see the need and do nothing. The Samaritan, on the other hand, bound up his wounds and took him to a hostel. We read in the Gospel that he took care of him. He took care *of* him because he had care *for* him. "He had compassion," Jesus said. And compassion is

54

never static. Christlike compassion is always active. It does not look to the other side when a wanting soul hungers or hurts. Compassion is pity that performs. It is mercy that moves. It is goodness grasping the hand of anyone in need and saying, "I am here."

While I was in college a famous lecturer came to address our assembly. He talked to us about a world that was in great need. He spoke briefly about why we should feed the people of India. As I recall, he felt several good things would result in such an enterprise. Our shipping vessels could employ men who were not then working. A bounty could be paid for the privilege of shipping through alien waters thus insuring friendly relations. Finally, we would be assured of continued good terms with the Indian people for our act of charity. "For these reasons," he suggested, "we should feed the people of India." During an informal discussion after the assembly, our oldest and most revered professor asked the guest speaker a question I have never forgotten. "Doctor," he inquired, "don't you think maybe we ought to feed them because they are hungry?"

This seems to be the reason that the young church in Acts formed its first committee of concern.

II

Let us consider the credentials that the twelve felt serving tables required. "Look out seven of your own number," they said to the rest of the disciples, "men of good reputation who are full of the Spirit and of wisdom." (Acts 6:3

55

Moffatt.) Had this duty been unimportant the twelve would never have been so strict in demanding such qualifications.

The first requirement was a good reputation. They would have to please both Hebrew and Hellenist. Only a man whose character was known and whose witness was trusted would be acceptable. And yet it is somewhat bewildering today to see men whose reputations are rather questionable serving in responsible positions. Yes, and some in places of religious authority. How vital it is that one at a spiritual station be living the kind of life no one can dispute.

One of my closest friends was once a star athlete at one of our largest Southern universities. All through his collegiate career he held the Christian banner high. He was nicknamed "Clean" by his teammates. Had he not been accorded their keenest respect he would never have been elected captain of the squad or president of the varsity club.

There is a spotlight that shines on all true followers of Christ. Remember people are constantly looking at you. Even some whom you may think have no intention of ever living the Christ-life are watching your actions and hearing your words. It is at the same time amazing and marvelous how a dedicated person can be pointing others to the Cross without even being aware of it.

"He made me a Christian," said Henry Stanley of David Livingstone, "and he never knew he was doing it." But that kind of influence is possible only when a man is allowing Christ to make him pure.

The second qualification was to be filled with the Spirit.

You may be thinking that surely this stipulation should be reserved for those in more effective areas of endeavor. "We will devote ourselves to prayer and to the ministry of the word." Here indeed the spirit must be present and powerful, but is there any great need for Spirit-fulness when it comes to table waiting? Well, the service we may consider ordinary becomes extraordinary in fact when our actions have been breathed upon by his holy Presence.

One of the seven men chosen for what I am certain many considered to be a menial vocation was Stephen. Now his attitude could have been far different than it was. He could have said, "I can't star, therefore I won't serve. I have not been chosen on the first string, therefore I'll not be a scrub. They won't let me pitch and so I won't play." I know some laymen who are like that. I know some ministers who share these same sentiments.

Jesus did not suggest to the disciples that the greatest among them would be the one who sparkled but the one who served.

What then was Stephen's response? Luke tells us that he performed great wonders and miracles among the people. But before that we read this phrase, "Stephen, full of grace and spiritual power." (Acts 6:8 Phillips.) Stephen would never have set Jerusalem afire with his heroic witness had he not been possessed by the Spirit. It is altogether possible that his triumphant death contributed more toward the conversion of Paul than any other thing. Yet he, who lived so grandly (the Sanhedrin saw that his face shone "like the face of an angel") and preached so powerfully and died so victoriously, served tables.

"If I have done anything of note," said General Booth humbly, "it is because the Holy Spirit has owned all of me." That could have been the testimony of Stephen. He was "filled through all his being with the Holy Spirit," translates Phillips. (Acts 7:54.)

Elton Trueblood is right in affirming, "We make a witness by telling not *who* we are but *whose* we are."

The final qualification was that those who served the tables be men of wisdom. It was not enough that they be righteous. Since seven were appointed, no doubt each would assume responsibilities for a day! They had to be men who knew how to meet these responsibilities, men who could discern actual needs and be both unselfish and temperate, since doubtless there was no surplus food supply. If there is a great demand for spiritual men, there is also great need for sensible men in the work of the Kingdom.

When Dwight L. Moody requested Henry Drummond to come to this country and give Bible lectures, Drummond did not accept the invitation immediately. He wrote Moody that his teaching might not be considered orthodox since he believed there were two Isaiahs. The evangelist speedily replied that he hasten on for most Americans did not even know there was one Isaiah. Thus in this particular instance practical judgment was every bit as important as religious devotion.

The Master considered such a requirement valid. He told a story about a rich man who had a dishonest agent.

When ordered to produce his stewardship accounts he quickly decided on his plan of action: One by one he called in his employer's debtors and charged them less than they owed. Thus he purchased their kindly feelings while at the same time he financially injured his employer. Now, our Lord certainly did not relate this parable as a guide to dishonesty. He only wants us to resemble this steward in his resourcefulness, his alertness to get what he wants done. "The children of this world are considerably more shrewd in dealing with their contemporaries than the children of light." (Luke 16:8 Phillips.)

III

What happened as a result of the selection of the seven? Here is Moffatt's translation: "The word of God spread; the number of the disciples . . . greatly increased, and a host of priests became obedient to the faith." (Acts 6:7.) Let us examine these separately.

The Word of God spread. When we read that, we are inclined to say of course. The Word of God spread because the disciples were relieved of some of their obligations. Hence, there were more people available to dispense the Word. That is true. Yet there is a sublime overtone here which we cannot afford to miss. It was the selflessness of the food distributers that gave the Word distributors their opportunity. Perhaps some of the seven felt they had been called to proclaim the Gospel in similar fashion. Be that as it may, they unselfishly gave of their energy to the task their brothers assigned. If it takes genuine consecration to attempt a superior duty in the King's service, it requires no less dedication to attend to what the world may call an inferior commission, for Jesus' sake.

Do you recall that memorable Old Testament scene when Jonathan went to David in the wilderness at Horesh? David was attempting to get away from Jonathan's father, Saul, who meant to kill him. "Fear not," Jonathan told David. "You shall be king over Israel, and I shall be next to you." (I Sam. 23:17.) This we are told strengthened David's hand in God.

Now, if it required devotion to God on David's part to become king, it required as much or more devotion on Jonathan's part to step aside and take second place. I have a friend who calls Jonathan, "The uncrowned king." If he never wore the kingly robe, he most assuredly owned a kingly soul.

So consecrated was Stephen to the task of table-waiting that the Holy Spirit used his voice to perform miracles among the people. And though there were those who disputed the truth that he preached, we read that they could not stand up against the spiritual force with which he spoke. He was distributing more than simply bread for physical existence to the needy. He was delivering the very bread of life, the manna from heaven, for which their spirits yearned. No wonder the Word of God spread!

The second point of consequence follows in direct line. The number of disciples greatly increased. Those who were proclaiming the Word were doing so with sincerity and faith. Those who were serving tables wore the same credentials of commitment. God will not fail to bless his Word whether it is declared in preaching or demonstrated in living. People were won into the Kingdom by hearing the gospel powerfully preached by the ministers. They were won into the Kingdom by seeing the gospel faithfully lived by the seven.

How is the Holy Spirit able to use us to enlist disciples for him? By surrendering our talents? That comes second. The first step is declaring our faith.

Four men brought a paralytic to Jesus and the Master healed him. But it seemed there was nothing the sick man did in order to be cured. Rather, the emphasis is on the men who carried him to Jesus. The Gospel account does not say that when Jesus observed their talent he made the man well. Neither does the Scripture relate that when he heard their preaching he forgave the man and sent him home. It says, "When Jesus saw their faith." (Matt. 9:2.)

When the author of Hebrews has finished calling the roll of the valiant, he adds this thrilling postscript, "All these won a glowing testimony to their faith." (Heb. 11:39 Phillips.)

The final effect was that a host of priests became obedient to the faith. This was the greatest miracle of all. This is the only time Luke ever records such a thing happening. Some of the priests may have been the ones directly responsible for Christ's death. Concerning this, we cannot be certain. But of one thing we are sure. Here is the one

61

occasion in the book of Acts when the priests who had objected so strongly to Christ, his men, and his message made any kind of sympathetic response to the gospel. "A host of priests became obedient to the faith." Just that one line is all we know but there seems to be so much else hinted there. The fact that this experience occurred at all indicates that many other things may have taken place.

Some of the priests at last got through the law to love. Some of these violently opposed to the Way opened their minds to understanding and their hearts to the Spirit and when they did the walls of tradition crumbled and the barriers of legalism fell. Perhaps those men who had actually judged Christ now believed him. Men who had ridiculed Christ now received him. Men who had hated him now followed him. "A host of priests became obedient to the faith."

Here is a rabbi. He is a deeply religious man. So devoted is he to the Jewish faith that he becomes the arch-persecuter of the Christians who challenge the older way. Then one day, as he travels the Damascus road for the purpose of continuing the persecution, he has an encounter that makes his entire life different. He meets personally the Lord Jesus Christ and is changed from Saul to Paul. "I was not disobedient to the heavenly vision," he said. Obeying that vision became the supreme motive of his life.

The Spirit of Christ is witnessing to countless millions today, many to whom he testifies are ministers. He wills that we obey him completely. These antagonistic priests of the long ago were transformed into obedient disciples when they heard the gospel proclaimed by witnesses and when they saw the gospel practiced by waiters. If you will faithfully obey the task he assigns, however great or small that responsibility may be, your life too will be a revelation of his presence.

VI
SONS OF
ENCOURAGEMENT

*They sent Barnabas to Antioch. When he arrived and saw
the divine grace at work, he rejoiced, and encouraged them
all to hold fast to the Lord.* —ACTS 11:22-23 *NEB*

The gospel of Barnabas was a gospel of encouragement.
His life, of course, made possible the good cheer he pro-
claimed. The name given to him by his parents was Joseph.
But the disciples as they saw him in action and were rallied
by his presence gave him a new name. They called him
"Son of encouragement."

If we are not men of hope who preach a message of hope then we have no right to affirm that we are Christ's witnesses.

Some time ago I heard the minister in the largest church of a certain denomination in a Southern state say that it may already be too late for the gospel to redeem society. If I believed that I should never enter the pulpit again. Such preaching is not only discouraging; it is unchristian.

The night our Lord was betrayed he looked out on a world that seemingly had lost all trace of the Father and said, "Be of good cheer, I have overcome the world."

After Barnabas went to Antioch we read that "large numbers were won to the Lord." (NEB.) This was a glorious added attraction. Barnabas had been sent not primarily to help in the ministry of conversion but consecration. The church had started in Antioch after the death of Stephen. The dispersed followers of Christ had gone there and preached gallantly. Barnabas came to Antioch to help these new disciples to grow and be steadfast, to "encourage them all to hold fast to the Lord."

This encouragement was contagious. When those who were not true followers of Jesus saw such resolute living they too came to the Savior. It is amazing what an encouraged disciple can do for a discouraged world by the influence of his life.

Listen to the report of a Boston newspaper: "It was a dull rainy day when things looked dark and lowering, but Phillips Brooks came down through Newspaper Row and all was bright."

65

How our pathetic, pessimistic old world needs the encouragement of godly lives and witnesses. Why was Barnabas able to do such a great work in Antioch? What enabled him to offer the encouragement they needed?

I

Barnabas was beautifully unselfish.

One reason why Luke could say there was not a needy person in the young Christian community was because of a great soul like Barnabas. We read that he sold his farm and brought the money to the apostles. Thus his unselfishness is shown first by what he was willing to do for others.

We are living in a contribution-conscious age. We measure nearly everything in terms of results. I think often how good it is to know that our Lord does not only judge the result but the intent. Man sees the end but God sees the aim. Do you recall what God said to David? "Whereas it was in your heart to build a house for my name, you did well that it was in your heart." (I Kings 8:18.)

Yet there are times when only achievement is helpful and only deeds are redemptive. Jesus did not say, "Blessed are the peace conceivers," or "Blessed are the peace advocates." He said, "Blessed are the peacemakers."

Barnabas did more than see the want of the young Christian community. He did more than sympathize with them in an hour of privation. He "brought the money and laid it at the apostles' feet."

A little chap dropped his sack of eggs as he was walking

home from the store. Tears and yolks immediately mingled together on the sidewalk. "I am so sorry, son, that you have had an accident," said a man and hurriedly passed by. "I trust things don't go hard for you at home," said a woman as she too hastened on her way. But another person passing that way stopped and did more than express regret or utter words of hope. "I care fifty cents' worth what happens to that lad," he said. Then he bought the boy another dozen eggs.

Jesus told a story about a shepherd who lost one of his sheep. He doesn't say that the shepherd worried over how pathetically lonely the lamb must have been. Nor does the Scripture inform us that he was concerned about how terribly cold he may have gotten. Doubtless both of these concerns were present. But he went out searching for that lost sheep until he found it.

I know of no sadder words that ever came from the lips of our Lord than these: "You refuse to come to me that you may have life." The unselfishness of Barnabas is seen in this fact: He came—he acted; he did something for Christ and for the Lord's needy.

But if the unselfishness of Barnabas was illustrated by what he could do, his devotion was evidenced by another fact. He was glad because of what others could do. When he saw the results of the labors of those first ministers to Antioch he rejoiced.

We do not know the names of the men that first delivered the gospel tidings to Antioch. But of this fact we are cer-

tain. There was a mighty response to the salvation message—a great many "turned to the Lord."

How human it would have been for Barnabas to have
resisted the Spirit guidance of the church when he was
commissioned to go to Antioch. He could have said, "Since
I was not sent to win them, I refuse to go and instruct
them." But he didn't. He was only glad because of what
others through the power of the Spirit had been able to
accomplish.

Paul witnessing to the Corinthians said: "Love knows
no jealousy." (Moffatt.)

"Paul," I question, "do you mean that? Perhaps you are
simply saying this because it sounds religious. Have you
proved it in your own ministry?"

His reply is, "I planted, Apollos watered, but God gave
the growth. So neither he who plants nor he who waters
is anything, but only God."

This was the way Barnabas felt except that he expressed
more joy over the pioneer efforts of the planters.

II

Barnabas was a man of great faith. This is indicated by
the men he helped. Look, for instance, at Paul and Mark.

Now the disciples found it difficult to believe that this
man Paul had really been converted. They had known
him as a persecutor. They could not imagine him as a
preacher. They had seen him cast their brothers into prison.

They had heard how he had voted for the death penalty. Perhaps even now they felt that he was seeking by pretext to do to death those who were leaders of the Way.

But Barnabas had seen Paul in action. He had heard him preach in Damascus with conviction and boldness that could not be doubted. Therefore, we read that "Barnabas . . . took him by the hand," (Phillips) and led him into the confidence of the early church.

I remember how surprised I was one evening to see a faithful Christian leading a certain man to our evening church service. He was not a questionable character. There was no question about it. Everyone that knew him knew he had been notoriously no good. But there was also no question about the one that brought him to our fellowship. We knew his life and witness. So when he said simply, "My friend has received Christ as his Savior," we knew that he had.

If Paul had been an antagonist who had changed, John Mark was a coward who needed to be changed. When he tells in his Gospel about a young man that ran away from the garden the night Jesus was arrested, it is altogether probable that he was writing about himself.

And when he journeyed with Paul and Barnabas to Perga, we read this disappointing commentary regarding his contribution there: "John left them and went back to Jerusalem" (Acts 13:13 Moffatt).

After this example of cowardice, Paul would not trust him enough to take him on the next missionary adventure. Again Barnabas comes forward to reassure with faith and Luke says simply, "Barnabas took Mark." So! Barnabas took Paul. Barnabas took Mark. What a "Son of encouragement"!

Later Simon Peter would mean a great deal in the life of Mark. But it is doubtful that he would ever have attempted a comeback after proving so spineless had not Barnabas stood by him. It may have been the confidence of Barnabas that opened the door to John Mark's genuine commitment. The trust we place in a man often means the difference between victory and defeat for his life.

Dr. Fosdick once told about a young businessman whose employment took him to Panama. Away from his family, he soon developed a laxness in character. His superior, who evidently was a very wise man, sent for him. The young man went to the conference much afraid. He knew he was worthy of dismissal. One who heard the conclusion of the interview reported this conversation: "Son," said the chief, "we are not going to drink anymore, are we?" "No, sir," the young man replied, "we are not." "And each week we are going to send so much money back to the wife and children, aren't we?" "By heaven, sir," he answered, "we will!"

It was Christ's confidence in men that made them. "You are Simon," he said. " 'You shall be called Cephas,' (that is, Peter, the Rock)." (John 1:42 NEB.)

Barnabas had faith very much akin to his Lord. Out of such trust many sons of encouragement may yet be born.

III

Barnabas was a man who was (to use Luke's phrase) "full of the Holy Spirit."

No experience in his ministry exemplifies this better than that which occurred at Lystra. As a result of the healing ministries of Paul and Barnabas there, the crowds complimented them in the highest way they knew. They called them by the names of the gods of Olympus. They called Barnabas Zeus and Paul Hermes.

But rather than honoring them this appears to have distressed them more than any response that could have been made. "Men . . . ." they cried, "We are only human beings, no less mortal than you. The good news we bring tells you to turn from these follies to the living God." (Acts 14:15 NEB.)

I fear there have been times in my own ministry when I have sought the honor for myself instead of for my Lord. I have to be in sympathy with this story which I heard recently.

"There is our minister," whispered a layman pointing to his pastor. "I tell you, he is invincible." Temporarily believing such flattery the proud preacher forgot his source of power. He found after a brief season of fruitless endeavor how utterly futile his efforts were unless touched by the Holy Spirit. A bit later he gave this testimony in the form of a confession, "My ministry began anew when I died to my invincibility."

The experience at Lystra is a pretty good test of how

pure a man's heart is. Barnabas did not want the praise he knew God should be accorded. The only hope for a sinful world to be lifted and blessed lies in the complete self-giving of the church as we point men only to Christ.

> He held the lamp that Sabbath day
> So high that none could miss the way,
> And yet so low to bring in sight
> That picture fair of Christ the Light,
> That, gazing up, the lamp between,
> The hand that held it scarce was seen. [1]

That is gospel preaching and Christian living at its radiant best.

Two men went to hear Charles H. Spurgeon preach. One in particular had waited long for such an opportunity. After the worship hour they walked in quiet for some little while before either of them spoke. Finally one turned to the other and asked, "Well, what did you think of Spurgeon?" His companion who had anticipated the service so long turned an astonished face to his friend. "Good heavens," he replied, "I was not even conscious of seeing him or hearing him. He made Christ so real I declare to you I could not even tell how the man Spurgeon looked or sounded."

I am certain the dedication of Barnabas caused such a holy impression. This privilege is possible for each one of us the more we are emptied of self and the more we are filled with his Presence.

[1] W. G. Elmslie, "The Hand That Held It."

VII
TURNING
BACK

Then Paul and his companions set sail from Paphos and went to Perga in Pamphylia. There John left them and turned back to Jerusalem. —ACTS 13:13 *Phillips*

"John . . . turned back." There is the touch of disaster in this brief sentence. It speaks of disaster for John Mark because of the golden hours he missed in the company of Paul and Barnabas. But if there is disaster in the missed blessing there is perhaps even greater tragedy in the neglected service.

73

The early church found it extremely difficult to make much progress in Pamphylia. This was true for at least two reasons. First, the climate was nothing short of deadly. Malaria was not unique in this district. If this made life hazardous for the native, one may clearly imagine what it might do for a tourist who was not accustomed to the region.

In the second place, Perga, the chief city of Pamphylia, was a center of pagan worship. Artemis, the pagan goddess of nature, had little competition for affection. She was known as "queen of Perga."

It was to this city that Paul and Barnabas and Mark felt directed by the Spirit. What eagerness Mark might have shared in this perilous mission! What youthful fervor he might have added to this dangerous assignment! Instead he left. He went back to Jerusalem.

I

Why did John Mark turn back?

Why do so many of us turn back?

One reason may be because *our faith is not deep enough.* We read this gloomy word in the Gospel of John: "From that time many of his disciples went back, and walked no more with him. (John 6:66 KJV.) To what time does this refer? Earlier Jesus had healed a man on the sabbath. The scribes and Pharisees could tell even in the beginning of his ministry that his emphasis was not one of law but life.

74

Perhaps some of his disciples went back because they did not believe in his principles.

Then, too, Jesus had already spoken of his atonement. Most of his followers were anticipating a conquering ruler not a crucified Redeemer. It is almost certain that more than a few deserted when a Cross was forecast for his ministry.

Finally it is altogether possible that some had never had complete confidence in him even at the start of his mission. Jesus preached only one sermon in his home synagogue and the congregation wanted to kill him. The reason may have been because they were so utterly wrapped up in themselves that they never attempted to focus their entire belief upon Jesus. The walls of self-esteem must crumble before Christ takes constant residence in the heart. This is primary.

Another reason that perhaps many of us turn back is because *our knowledge is not clear enough.* This knowledge of which we speak is more than believing. It also means belonging. Paul could think of no higher goal for the Christian than knowing Christ "and the power of his resurrection [and the fellowship of] his sufferings." I wonder if these are not the two ways we need to know him and yet miss knowing him today. Let us look at these two points a moment.

We need to know him as suffering Redeemer. When the Master first outlined his mission as martyr, Peter rebuked him. Perhaps this was the reason he later denied him—he was not willing to ally himself with a cause offering Calvary to those who knew Jesus.

Now the Master's cross-bearing call to discipleship was directed not just to Simon and the other eleven. "If any one wants to follow in my footsteps" (Phillips), he said. If we do not answer the call to follow a redeeming Savior then we do not answer. If we do not come pledged to the fellowship of his sufferings then we do not come at all. "I bear on my body the marks of Jesus," said Paul. That is knowledge that is clear.

We need to know Christ not only as suffering Redeemer but as living Lord. This is the certainty that crowns our faith. When Thomas saw Christ alive, he did not need to touch him. He said only, "My Lord and my God." Thomas had accepted him as Master. Then his faith, as did the faith of the others, weakened. Now he knew Christ as the Eternally Living God. Such knowledge is available for all who come with hearts of faith.

This faith gives us also the assurance of eternal life and we sing joyfully:

> We feel the resurrection near,
> Our life in Christ concealed,
> And with His glorious presence here
> His life in us revealed.
> —CHARLES WESLEY

In an old cemetery in the south of England there is a headstone so defaced that the name on it can scarcely be read. There are some words on it, however, that have not been worn beyond recognition by the passing of the years.

"Gone away with a friend," can still be deciphered. Again, this is knowledge that is clear.

I strongly suspect the biggest reason we turn back from following Christ is because *our dedication is not great enough.* This, I think, was the basis for Mark's unfaithfulness.

There is little doubt but that he had already proved cowardly in time of stress. His Gospel relates how a young man followed Jesus after his arrest in the garden. Suddenly he was discovered but escaped before he could be apprehended. In all probability he was writing about himself.

Mark was still young. His heart was still fearful. The foes of the gospel crusaders were many. They were mocked. They were threatened. They were imprisoned. Perhaps they would even be killed for declaring their faith. Only recently James had died a martyr's death.

So Mark stood at the crossroads in Perga. Of course there was danger back in Jerusalem, but at least the movement was respected there, and had gained considerable following. And there were many of their own number upon whom he could lean. But here was a society that was alien and a religion that was pagan. So Mark counted the cost and decided he was not willing to pay the price.

Many stand at the crossroads today. The biggest obstacle that faces us is not the presence of doubt but the absence of devotion. There are those who have intellectual problems. But the most of us fail to rally to Christ's call not because the mind lacks comprehension but because the soul lacks commitment.

A scribe once came to Jesus and promised to follow him. The Lord answered, "Foxes have holes, and birds of the air have nests; but the Son of man has nowhere to lay his head." If that scribe became a disciple we know nothing about it. Why did he fail to follow Christ? It was not because of the mental difficulty in believing the subterranean habits of the fox. Nor was there any great problem connected with the consideration of the receptacle prepared by the birds for their young. He did not follow because he did not dare.

So if there are those who fail to start because of the lack of dedication there are those who fail to continue for the same reason.

"You are those who have continued with me in my trials." That was how our Lord addressed himself to the disciples in that last Upper Room intimacy. Dedication had done it. Dedication will do it.

II

We have been seeking an answer to the question, Why do men turn back. We come now to the second inquiry of moment; namely, how do men turn back?

It is doubtful if the backsliding process consists of one fell swoop. True, there may be giant steps that make betrayal possible. It is my observation, however, that a soul is slow in dying. Visions must perish and dreams must fade, ideals vanish and high expectations depart. It is not an easy victory for the forces of darkness. Evil convicts but so does righteousness, and the good seldom exists without a struggle.

Let us then suggest three losses that make for spiritual shipwreck.

1. We lose our interest in the higher way. This may come about by our failure to practice the holy habit of prayer. Or we allow our Bibles to gather dust on the shelf instead of opening them to receive guidance and strength. Or the church no longer holds a position of prominence in our affection. Or we no longer give evidence of our faith by our witness. We may ignore all of these roads to deeper dedication by our supreme refusal to seek first his Kingdom and his righteousness. God does not mean everything to us.

A newly appointed minister stood in front of his congregation one Sunday morning for the first time. "I will ask you three questions," he said. "How you answer these questions will determine the impact our church has upon the community. Is Jesus *nothing* to you? Is Jesus *something* to you? Is Jesus *everything* to you?" In my opinion that church today is the greatest single force in the city because of its interest in seeking first the Kingdom.

Any church—any group—any individual that fails to give God initial interest has already started the downward trek. Look at two examples of this. One is found in the Old Testament and one in the New. These illustrations are of men who lost interest in the *primacy* of God. They are alike, too, in the fact that each walked in the company of a great friend who chose the higher path. Lastly, they resemble in the donation that their lives ultimately made.

Lot and Abraham stood between Bethel and Ai with

Lot given preference as to which land should be his. Is not this phrase significant? "Lot chose for himself all the Jordan valley." As a result of choosing for himself, Lot lost his hold on God. Though he escaped Sodom when it was destroyed we wonder in reading of his later life if the best in him had not died when he left the highlands of Haran. On the other hand Abraham discussed his choice with the Lord and built an altar to him when he came to his settling place.

Paul once referred to Demas as his "fellow worker." Evidently he meant much to the Apostle. He could have meant even more to him while he was shut up in a Roman prison. His contribution to the young Christian movement might have been of great import. Instead Paul writes, "Demas, in love with this present world, has deserted me."

2. We lose our enthusiasm. Read again Paul's words to the Romans, "Maintain the spiritual glow" (Rom. 12:11 Moffatt). If we are to know religion at its radiant best, we must sustain the fervor of a constantly devoted heart. There is only one kind of sanctification and that is daily sanctification.

There are many more days of sunshine than shadows. How marvelous is the itinerant road! Yet there is one recurring heartbreak that never ceases to bring distress and that is to see the fire of a soul go out. God help pastor and people to keep the flame of the spirit burning!

A district superintendent in The Methodist Church waited upon a pastoral relations committee. "We want a man," they said, "who has not let the new wear off." "Oh," he responded, "then your church would like a young preacher." "It does not matter about his age," they answered, "so long as he has not let the new wear off."

I have known a few seminary men who would sputter and spat over theological differences and not cross the street to declare to some needy soul the tidings of great joy. I count it one of my choicest blessings to know some old soldiers of the Cross with grey on their heads and grace in their hearts who still travel as God's ambassadors looking up and lifting up. They have not let the new wear off.

I do not think the laity is a great deal different. I have seen young people become old overnight when bitterness, cynicism, or jealousy invaded the sanctuary of their souls. I believe it was Nicholas Murray Butler who observed candidly that some die at twenty and wait until they are sixty to be buried.

There is a woman in my church who is ever girded with the new in Christ which our Lord gave to her many years ago as a young girl. Not long ago she said to me, "I fear my age and health will not permit me to come to church many more days. When I am no longer able to attend the services," she inquired, "would it be asking too much for you to come occasionally to my home and speak to me from his word and tell me of his love?"

There are many winsome wonders connected with the Christ-life. But I know of none so attractive as a Christian who for a life time has walked in the enthusiasm of a divine encounter.

3. Thus losing our interest and our enthusiasm it is not long until we lose our experience.

It was not simply money that led to the downfall of Judas. He first lost his interest in the kind of Kingdom Jesus proposed to build. He then lost his enthusiasm for the Architect who had come to lay its foundation. The loss of his dedication came then as a matter of course. He could hardly have done anything but betray his Lord. In fact, the deadly truth may be, when we finally recognize that our interest and zeal are missing, that even the consecration we thought we possessed will be gone.

But we can come back to God! Even after Judas betrayed Jesus he could have repented and returned. Mark betrayed Paul and Barnabas but he reversed the trail that led down and he began anew.

Paul, years later, wrote to Timothy. "Pick up Mark and bring him with you, for he is useful in helping me." (II Tim. 4:11 Moffatt.)

A young minister came to the altar one evening in apparent distress. He lingered until after the benediction. When he rose to leave his countenance was transformed. Gripping my hand tightly, he confided, "Wallace, I lost the high call from my soul. I found it again tonight."

No downfall need be decisive. No failure need be fatal. What you have lost you may find again—and more. The Holy Spirit is not simply waiting. He is seeking. He is yearning. He is urging that you respond.

VIII
RESPONSE TO THE RESURRECTION

"Now when they heard of the resurrection of the dead, some mocked; but others said, 'We will hear you again about this.'. . . But some men joined him and believed."—ACTS 17:32, 34

Though moving, the Lord's death on the cross would have meant but little, had there been no Easter Day. The common people who had heard him gladly would now have spoken wearily and sadly. They would have echoed the words of Cleopas, "We had hoped," but like a dying ember the fire that had burned would soon have been extinguished completely and permanently.

Those closest to our Lord would for a while have whispered wistfully in the shadows about a Lord who never returned and a Kingdom that never came. But within a handful of years the name "Jesus," if not utterly forgotten, would have been scarcely more than a cynic's joke or a Jew's scorn.

But he did come back! He walked from the tomb alive forevermore! Now the greatest testimony the Holy Spirit gives is offering to men the opportunity to experience a living Christ. "Jesus Christ of Nazareth, whom you crucified," declared Peter after Pentecost, ". . . God raised from the dead."

It is important to note, however, that in giving this witness of a resurrected Lord, the Spirit through Simon is but bearing testimony of himself. The Holy Spirit is Christ alive within the heart. Thus as Paul preaches the Resurrection in the city of Athens, he is proclaiming to them the gospel of the Spirit. The Athenian response to the Resurrection is but an attitude toward the Divine Presence.

There were three definite reactions to the tidings that Paul delivered.

I

Some of the people of Athens mocked when they heard Paul witness about the resurrection of the dead. What causes people to mock?

Some people mock because they do not understand. If

something is not clear to them then they hold it in contempt. Is not this a philosophy which is all too common? Either grasp an ideal or get rid of it. Jesus cured the demoniac of Gadara, but the people did not comprehend the wonder of this miracle. So what? They begged Jesus to go elsewhere. Perhaps this was the reason for the derision Paul received at Athens in response to his preaching concerning the dead being raised.

Others mock because they do not believe. Those who watched Christ die cried in derision: "If you are the Son of God, come down from the cross." General Booth used to say, "We believe in him because he stayed up there." Those around the cross, however, not believing that Jesus was the Christ, merely mocked his redemptive act.

Then others mock what they are not willing to accept. Here are a group of men upon whom the Holy Spirit has fallen. Aflame with the new experience, they quickly began to testify concerning it. Many who were watching asked what this meant. The mockers present were ready with an immediate answer, "They are filled with new wine." One is tempted to add that if this were true it would certainly be good if we knew their brand. Not accepting Christ and his teachings about the promised gift, naturally they rejected the Spirit when he came and those to whom he came.

How do people mock?

Some mock with words. We are not told exactly what this segment of the crowd at Athens said to Paul when his sermon was concluded. We do not know if they heckled or hissed. Luke does not say whether they challenged or chided. But this we do know—their response was not favorable. "Some mocked." Our Lord placed great emphasis on the right way to speak. He said that words would justify or condemn us. I have seen more evil done by unrighteous talk than any other single thing.

Many times I have been tempted to offer a remedy like Bud Robinson, that quaint Nazarene preacher, offered one of his parishioners. "The whole trouble with my religious life," a woman confessed to him, "is my tongue. It is simply too long." Bud pointed toward the church altar and said, "That altar is thirty foot long. Won't that accommodate that tongue of yourn?"

There are those who mock with actions. Jesus told about a nobleman who gave twenty dollars to each of his servants with which to trade. When the day of reckoning came, one servant had earned two hundred dollars. A second had made one hundred dollars. But another simply laid his money away. He did not invest. He did not speculate. He did nothing. Why is this man condemned in the eyes of our Lord? Because he made a mock of his trust. He disappointed his confidant. We would do well to remember at this point that the word "mock" means to disappoint as well as deride.

What of these lives of ours? What of the talents we possess? A sinful race and a needy world cry out to God's children not for a seclusion but an invasion. When our church becomes more monastery than missionary we deserve to have our divine Investor say, "Take the pound from him and give it to the man with ten" (Luke 19:24 NEB).

God grant that in this day of moral apathy and spiritual inertia our religion shall not be a cloistered convent but a clarion command: "Go and make disciples of all nations."

Now what is the result of mocking? There are two basic effects, I think. The first is that we become bitter. I have never known a cynic that didn't earn his title by a lot of practice. When one sees only evil in others it cannot help but be that there is mostly evil in him. Jesus asked, "Why do you look at the speck of sawdust in your brother's eye, with never a thought for the great plank in your own?" (Luke 6:41.) It is not difficult to locate some specks if you go looking for them. All of us have them. But how terribly sad it is to be such dirt diggers and filth finders that people recognize us by our sneers.

The second consequence of mocking is that we lose any chance we might have of contributing something fine to the world. If you are bitter you have nothing to share but bitterness. I have seen the cynic convert his prey. How tragic it is and how terribly contagious it is. "Those who passed by derided him. . . . So also the chief priests, with the scribes and elders, mocked him. . . . And the robbers reviled him in the same way." (Matt. 27:39-44.) One can be led to the better way by Christ's soldiers, but one can also be led to the bitter way by his scoffers.

II

Then others after hearing of the Resurrection that day in Athens said, "We will hear you again about this." If there were those present who mocked, there were also those present who postponed. I am afraid that I have known many who though not scoffing when the Holy Spirit sought access into the citadel of their soul simply put him off. Why do people do this?

Some procrastinate because they say *they are not worthy.* If this is a sincere reason and not just a flimsy excuse, I have perhaps more hope for one who offers it than one who gives any other explanation.

God can never enter the heart that feels it deserves his admission. "I thank thee that I am not like other men," prayed the Pharisee, and he went to his house with pride. "God, be merciful to me a sinner!" prayed the tax collector, and he went to his house with pardon.

Just for sheer dedication, with the possible exception of Jeremiah, Isaiah stands as the supreme prophet of the Old Testament. Whence the power of his prophetic lips? The initial reason was the confession that those lips were unclean. "Woe is me!" he prayed. "For I am lost." When one thus pours out his soul to God and accepts his forgiveness, he can testify, "Happy am I, for I am saved."

When a man says to me that he is not worthy, I say to him that it is for his sake that Christ came. The Incarnation was not for the morally perfect but for the lost sheep of the house of Israel, not only for the socially decent but for the degenerate and forgotten. It was not primarily for the spiritually respected but for those who need a Savior. And you must remember that he did not come to a castle but a manger. He did not serve a respectable pulpit but he walked an itinerate road. He did not call only for the rich and influential and powerful, but he said, "Come to me, all who labor and are heavy-laden, and I will give you rest." And when he died, it was not in the ease of luxury but in the pain of Calvary.

To the lonely and sinful and unworthy we are privileged to present this glorious news—his own words: "The Son of man came to seek and to save the lost."

Then there are those who say *they are not convinced.* I think this was the reason Paul's message was deferred by some of the people in Athens. Religion's main forte in that city appeared to be not inspiration but inspection, not dedication but deliberation.

Actually the only reason Paul was invited to preach in the Areopagus was not because he proclaimed something great but something new. This strange unique doctrine about the Resurrection might have afforded a field day for the Athenian philosophers except for one thing. Paul did not debate it. He declared it. He did not examine. He exhorted.

The service, however, ended without an altar call. In fact, it broke up before the sermon was concluded. The distinction between preacher and congregation at this point was simply too great. Here sits an assembly that favors speculative conferences and here stands an evangelist who wants spiritual commitments and the chasm is just too wide.

So this service at Athens became Paul's unfinished symphony and he had to lay the baton down. I think he felt his ministry failed here because he never finished that sermon. In my opinion had he not been interrupted, the Cross would most certainly have been lifted, salvation would have been stressed, and the joy of the Christ-life would have been declared. Even so there was enough gospel to get some to Christ that day.

But others were not persuaded. Perhaps they did not want to be convinced. No doubt that was true concerning many of them. I cannot help but feel, however, that there were some in that assembly who longed for what this strange enthusiastic preacher said to be so. For though we have those superficial ridiculous critics of the faith we have also those wistful longing souls who yearn for what we say to be true.

James S. Stewart in *Heralds of God* says: "No man's soul can be satisfied indefinitely with the wretched husks of a materialist philosophy. It begins to starve for something better than such poor earthy stuff. Sooner or later, the famine grips it. It grows homesick. . . . It wants to fling its windows open toward Jerusalem. It cries aloud for the God who is its home."

This then is our great commission and privilege. But the resurrected Lord, the alive Christ, the Holy Presence must be real in our lives before we can win those who seek great conviction. Describing the impression John Brown made upon him, David Hume said, "He speaks as if Jesus was at his elbow." That is the way we must talk and act if we are to claim the world. There is no other way.

There exists a third group which claims *they are not able*. To them I simply say neither am I. And neither was Paul, but he was "perfectly certain that the work" God committed to him is safe in God's hands. (II Tim. 1:12 Phillips.) Peter felt this same way, for he said: "You, because you put your faith in God are under the protection of his power" (I Pet. 1:5 NEB). So! He keeps! He protects! We are not able. If we think we are, we have lost the battle before we even start the good fight. But he is able. That was the declaration of the three young Jews who faced a fiery death if they did not deny their religion. "Our God . . . is able," they said. That is how the dynamic, youthful church of the book of Acts faced any difficulty, endured any hardship, suffered any loss. The Holy Spirit—Christ within—made them able. And victorious!

"Daddy," said a little four-year-old girl, "I am so tired of walking." Indeed the parking lot did seem farther away than when they had parked the car and made their shopping trek earlier. "I am going to let go of your hand and you hold on to mine." That is how we can travel life's highroad with certainty! We are his disciples but not primarily because we are holding on to God but because God is holding on to us.

What a marvelous benediction that is in the letter of Jude. It begins, "Now to him who is able to keep you from falling." But you say it is too difficult; as long as I am in sin I can't stand. Yes, but as long as you are in Christ, you can't fall. Lean your weak shoulder then upon this strong fact: He is able.

Finally, there are those who say *they are not ready*. Now it is so easy to rationalize here. It is probably true that intel-

91

lectual doubts kept some of the Athenians from spiritual certainty. But even so, could this not have been because they did not dare ally themselves with that which seemed too amazing, too miraculous, too good to be true? "When they heard about the raising of the dead," they said, "We will hear you on this subject some other time." Acts 17:32 NEB).

Now they may have meant by this only to retard. But they may have meant to completely reject. For what we delay for the sake of tomorrow, we are denying for the sake of today. It is easy for us to seemingly have a conditional motive on our lips when there is an absolute refusal in our hearts. I am not dogmatic in this assertion. I am but suggesting that such may have been the case.

In point of fact, look at Thomas. He was not present when the Lord appeared to the other disciples. When they told him they had seen the risen Christ he answered, "Unless I see in his hands the print of the nails, and place my finger in the mark of the nails, and place my hand in his side, I will not believe." In reality, he meant by this statement that regardless of their testimony he would not accept it.

If these Athenians had received the truth they would no longer have had to carry on their fruitless and futile consultations. If Thomas had believed the truth, he would have spared himself more than a week of misery and heartache.

The time that the Bible wants us to be receivers of his blessings is always now. If we should ask Paul when to

92

decide to live for Christ, he would say, "Now is the acceptable time; behold, now is the day of salvation" (II Cor. 6:2). If we should ask Joshua when to resolve that we are going to be servants of the most high God, he would say, "Choose to-day" (Josh. 24:15 Moffatt).

When are we to petition him? "Give us today our daily bread." (Matt. 6:11 NEB.) When are we to praise him?

This is the day which the Lord has made;
let us rejoice and be glad in it." (Ps. 118:24.)

And when we die, when are we to be restored to his presence? "Today you will be with me in Paradise." (Luke 23:43.)

III

Some mocked, some said, "We will hear you again." Here is the third reaction to the Resurrection; the living, indwelling Christ: "But some men joined him and believed."

I am so glad Luke tells us about this in the way that he did. They joined him and believed. It was not simply mental awareness but spiritual acceptance. What is involved here is not merely head knowledge but heart action. They believed *in* Christ but they did more. They belonged *to* Christ. Not only did they believe but they joined. I care little whether we enter the Kingdom head first or heart first. When asked the greatest commandment, Jesus answered, "Love the Lord your God with all your heart . . . and all your mind" in the same breath. Whichever comes first, they must surely blend together, if we are to have religion at its real and radiant best. Costen J. Harrell is right in affirming that education and evangelism are more than a corporation; they are a holy wedlock. Religion only of heart may be purely emotional and have no foundation upon which can be built more stately mansions. Religion only of head may be merely intellectual and have no incentive to lift up the fallen or redeem the unsaved.

Consider two men who were both failures. One is Felix, and the other is Simon the magician. Felix was mentally aware of religion. Luke says he had a rather accurate knowledge of the Way. But it was a knowledge of and not a sharing in, so how pitifully useless he was to the Kingdom. Simon, we are told by Luke, believed and was baptized. But when he saw the power of Spirit baptism, he thought what an exciting added attraction this would make to his magic show. So he offered the disciples money for such a gift. He was emotionally stirred but he did not allow religion to make him mentally sound.

"Pray for me, Chaplain," said a frightened young soldier on the eve of the battle. "I will pray for you," he said, "but I am going to go with you." That is the gospel our church must proclaim. This is the faith we Christians must live— prayer to God and service with God, awareness of him and action for him. With such dedication the scoffers and delayers, even the most prodigal of Athens, may yet believe and enlist.

94

IX
BUSY PREACHING

When Silas and Timothy arrived from Macedonia, Paul was occupied with preaching, testifying to the Jews that the Christ was Jesus. —ACTS 18:5

It may be that in the twentieth century the ministry has rationalized itself into believing that the task of preaching is secondary. Let us be concerned with organizing. Let us be engrossed with administrating. Let us be employed with visiting.

95

Now it is assuredly not my purpose to belittle these necessities. Organization keeps the machine rolling. Proper administration enables it to roll smoothly. Visitation helps carry its program into ever-widening areas. But it is preaching that fires up the engine.

I am not disregarding these other things. A minister's functions are varied. His duties are many. I am pleading, however, for what I believe to be our highest duty. Regardless of how versatile one is, he must have an emphasis. It is my earnest conviction that our main obligation is to declare the Word. When Silas and Timothy arrived in Corinth, they found Paul busy preaching. Now if it was Paul's task, it is no less ours.

I shall never forget how this impression was all but forced upon me. I was preparing to move from a rural charge that I had served several years. I invited four men to join with me in a discussion, the purpose being to decide what type of ministry they felt was needed in that particular section. Directly after our meeting, I was to have a conference with our district superintendent at which time I would relate the substance of our council.

I began by saying that I felt they needed a pastor who would major on visitation; one who would go to their homes, barns, and fields and carry the good news to all of that rural area. I was cut off almost immediately. "Brother Chappell," said one of the four farmers, "use your influence to help us get a preacher." The others nodded in agreement as he continued, "We can coax a man into visiting, but we can't teach a man to preach."

I must confess I gained nearly as much insight into our high calling during those few minutes with four uneducated farmers as I did in three years of seminary training. They felt one thing was essential above all others and they were quick to say so.

It was the supreme minister who said,

> The Spirit of the Lord is upon me,
> because he has anointed me to preach. (Luke 4:18.)

And it was his greatest witness, who in testifying of the divine decree, said, "He commanded us to preach" (Acts 10:42).

So! We are anointed for the purpose of preaching. We are commanded to accomplish that purpose. But for what reason? Why should we be occupied with preaching?

I

We should attend to the paramount task of preaching because *it is the way the Kingdom is inaugurated.*

We have just mentioned the text that our Lord used for his sermon at Nazareth. It was, of course, from Isaiah: "He [the Lord] has anointed me to preach." When he finished reading from the scroll, his initial word was, "Today . . . this text has come true" (Luke 4:21 NEB).

This fact is significant. Here at Nazareth we have our Lord's first public appearance in a rabbinic role. Note that he did not initiate his Messiahship by performing a sign but by preaching a sermon.

His manner was the same when he started his itinerant ministry through Galilee. Luke tells that "he went travelling from one town and village to another, preaching and telling the good news." (Luke 8:1 Moffatt.) Now if we as ambassadors for Christ really yearn to be like him, what better way is there than adapting the method he practiced!

Let us not commit error here. Our primary function is not to plan programs but to change lives. The program has already been planned. Some there are who seek to pull us astray of our major responsibility.

Once in a quiet place near Capernaum Jesus was getting a bit of rest. His peace, however, was disturbed by friendly folk who begged that he not continue his travel for the present. They urged him to abide with them. "I must preach the glad news to the other cities also," he told them, "for I was sent for this purpose."

I must confess that it convicts my soul when I see how often I have placed the main emphasis elsewhere. I have gone programming. I have gone managing. I have gone coordinating. All good. All necessary. But all secondary. What was it our Master did, Luke? "He went preaching." (Luke 4:44 Moffatt.)

Then we should be occupied with preaching because *it is the way the gospel is conveyed*. Receiving the good news is, thus, dependent upon two factors. First, there is the preacher who proclaims. It is impossible to receive a message without a messenger. When Paul was speaking to the Romans on the subject of salvation, he asked the query we are considering here. This was the question: "How are they [those without Christ] to hear without a preacher?"

As tremendous as this may seem, nevertheless, it is true that the effectiveness of the ministry of the Spirit is largely dependent upon the faithful witness of his ministers.

I am persuaded the entire service of the ministry would afford a higher intention and greater devotion if we would allow this momentous fact to lay hold of our hearts. The possibility is strong that the only chance our people will have of hearing God's good news is through us.

The second factor is the tidings we tell. If the courier is essential, the communication is none the less important. In fact, the gospel is a thousand times bigger than any spokesman who declares it. The evangel must be released by the evangelist. But if the man gives the message liberty it is the message that gives the man life. One of our greatest ministers refers to this association of message and messenger in this way: "Ideas that have used me."

How urgent it is that we have good news to relate. Here is the stress Paul placed upon it: "It pleased God through the folly of what we preach to save those who believe."

Some will no doubt say that we are not all called to promote evangelism. I can only answer that evangelism means the preaching of good news and if we fail to declare the evangel, then we are preaching bad news.

Then, *preaching is the method by which disciples are enlisted.* The Christian church never had a greater day of enlistment than Pentecost. Three thousand souls were brought in, translates Moffatt, and that is a powerful awakening!

How did it happen? The Holy Spirit moved mightily upon their hearts to be sure.

But here is the question to which we are giving our immediate attention. When did it happen? It occurred after Simon Peter had preached. Luke tells us that when they heard his sermon, "they were cut to the heart." Do you recall the last time you preached a sermon or heard a sermon that had such an effect?

It was my great privilege to study under Edwin Mims, that distinguished patriarch of English literature. I knew him as an old man. Yet he exhorted (and I know of no other way to describe his lectures) in the classroom with an enthusiasm that was as unrestrained as a spirited youngster announcing that school was out.

Dr. Mims and I were traveling together on one occasion and he was telling me something of the results he wished his instructions would have upon his students. "Often," he said, "one comes to me at the close of the period and says, 'I enjoyed your discussion.' I want to grab hold of him and say, 'Yes, yes, but did it change your life?' " If a man feels this way about an English lecture, how should we feel about the gospel message!

When Paul and Barnabas were preaching in Galatia, a tremendous revival broke out at Derbe. Luke says they had many converts. When did it happen? "After preaching the gospel to that town." (Acts 14:21 Moffatt.)

Oftentimes *preaching is the means by which the church is strengthened.* Luke gives some evidences to this fact. Paul "went through Syria and Cilicia, strengthening the churches." (Acts 15:41) Paul and Barnabas went to Antioch—the purpose of their mission to "put fresh heart into the disciples there, urging them to stand firm in the faith" (Acts 14:22 Phillips).

H. H. Farmer says that one of the basic reasons our preaching today is ineffective is because it lacks courage. There are people in our pews every Sunday who are being tempted to give up the fight. What audacious tact Satan uses here. He would never first of all suggest to a Christian that he should murder his neighbor or burgle his home or steal his wife. He whispers to us that we are too weak to walk the higher way. He makes us think the cost is too great. With brilliant subtleness he tells us we are not capable of carrying out errands of mercy for Christ. He knows that weakness is the open door to wickedness. He does not at the outset want us to admit that we are sinful enough to do wrong, only that, we are not strong enough to do right.

There is a tragic but true word in C. S. Lewis' *The Screwtape Letters* that is relevant. Wormwood is being admonished by Screwtape not to allow his candidate for hell to feel he can possess the courage of God. "Remember," he writes, "cowardice is all that matters."

The good news tells us we can go on. Jesus never said it would be easy. He never promised tasks without trials or blessings without burdens or crowns without crosses.

But he did promise to be with us always, never to fail or forsake us. If he said it to us, we can say it to others.

II

The second question is what kind of preaching should occupy our energy? I have three very simple suggestions.

We should proclaim messages that *interest.* We are seeking by the spoken word to initiate a Kingdom, spread good news, enlist disciples, and strengthen the church. But we must remember that it is attention that leads to action. Consecration depends upon concentration. Before one commits, he considers. Does our preaching command the interest of those to whom we speak?

One layman was brutally frank when he remarked that his minister was so dull he would give an aspirin a headache. Most of our ministers are men of high integrity and genuine dedication. The biggest foe of the pulpit is not badness. It is dullness.

A kind of radiant eagerness, a glad enthusiasm, should so accompany our message that the *way* we speak will complement the *words* we speak.

Can you imagine Paul standing before the Galatian church and saying in a dead drab tone, "I have been crucified with Christ: the life I now live is not my life, but the life which Christ lives in me" (Gal. 2:20 NEB)?

Could you picture Simon Peter looking out over that scattered flock in Asia Minor and reciting in a sluggish monotone these words: "You are . . . a people claimed by

God . . . to proclaim the triumphs of him who has called you out of darkness into his marvellous light" (I Pet. 2:9 NEB)?

At Pentecost when the disciples, thrilled by the Spirit, began telling the great things God had done, some of the Jews said with a sneer, "They have been drinking!" (Acts 2:13 NEB). After seeing and hearing men witness with such fervor, one can readily understand why Simon had little trouble securing the alertness of the crowd.

My friends who are laymen in our church could incriminate my preaching on many points, I fear, if they were so minded. But I doubt seriously if I have ever proclaimed Christ with such a flaming fervency as to make possible the accusation, "Our preacher is drunk."

I do not intend here that you think I am encouraging sensationalism. I certainly do not mean that you must shout wildly or lose yourself in an emotional frenzy. I am advocating a contagious zeal as we warmly witness of Jesus and his love.

Second, we should declare tidings that *instruct*. Doctrine does not need to be dull. Much of the church's theology is gleaned from Paul's epistle to the Romans. I am constantly moved to surrender and service as I read this tremendous little book. Theological though it be, it is difficult for me to see how a minister or layman can read the fifth, eighth, and twelfth chapters and not have their minds enlightened as well as their faculties commissioned.

If preaching theological sermons is becoming taboo in the modern pulpit, it may be because our terms are too technical. As ministers we will find an exciting and contributive work in making theological expressions living experiences for our people. After all, theology is but the skeleton and our sermons, if carefully prepared, can be the skin that gives firmness and purpose.

We must never fail to remember that a man cannot be helped by preaching unless he understands the sermon. Read again the Gospels and note the simplicity and practicality and yet the tremendous strength with which our Lord spoke.

Above all the preacher must properly instruct himself. "I study hard," a pre-med student said to me one day while I was attending seminary. "I hear men lecture all week who know their business. On Sunday I go to church and hear my pastor preach and if he has studied one whit, I cannot tell it. To be perfectly honest," he confessed, "I feel intellectually insulted." And I did not blame him.

The prime textbook for instructor and instructed is the Bible. "Read the Bible?" responded a minister in answer to a friend's question about his devotional habits. "Why I studied it in theology school. I am reading books now I have not read before."

How tragic! Whatever else we may preach that is good, if we leave his word out there will be little lasting significance to our ministry. "You search the scriptures," said Christ to the Jews, "because you think that in them you have eternal life; and it is they that bear witness to me."

To be sure this was an indictment *against* them, but had they allowed it it could have been a commission *for* them.

It is for us. The Word bears witness to Christ. Let us bear witness through the Word.

Third, we should preach sermons that *inspire*. If our messages are breathed upon by the Holy Spirit they will inspire.

They might inspire one to quit his sin. They might move one to assume more obligations in the Christian fellowship. They might lift another to grander and nobler living. Gospel preaching should not end when it interests us enough to *see* something and instructs us enough to *know* something. It must inspire us enough to *do* something.

"Preach to the heart," said Moody. And he preached to over a 100,000,000 of them. He personally pleaded with more than 750,000 people. He could preach to the heart because he preached from the heart.

Certainly they were cut to the heart on Pentecost day for the evangelist's own heart had been so inflamed and empowered by the Holy Spirit. That is witnessing at its best; Christ speaking to and through us. "Christ . . . lives in me," said Paul. "I . . . preach him among the Gentiles."

Several years ago I was preaching for a week at the United States Air Force Base in Madison, Wisconsin. One evening, not long before the mission concluded, a young corporal sang an anthem. He sang with great feeling and I remember that it moved me deeply. After the worship hour, we spoke together and I expressed my appreciation. "I am grateful if my contribution was helpful," he said. "But I could sing like I did because I had been hearing you preach like you did." It was not a winsome speaker, however, but the witnessing Spirit that was of benefit to the young flyer. That same blessed Spirit yearns to be a benediction to all the world. How many he can redeem and uplift depends in a large measure upon our being occupied with preaching.

X
A PASTOR
AND HIS PEOPLE

For I did not shrink from declaring to you the whole coun-
sel of God. —ACTS 20:27

This verse is taken from one of the most tender and one
of the most beautiful chapters in the New Testament.
Here at Miletus Paul is preaching to the Ephesian elders.
With the possible exception of the church at Philippi, it
is doubtful that the Apostle ever loved a congregation
as much as he loved his people in Ephesus. The fact that

he was exposed to great danger during his ministry there seems to have made their fellowship the more precious.

He was now on his way to Jerusalem. Luke tells us that he was in haste seeking to arrive on the day of Pentecost. At this point the critics have gone to great length to disprove the historical accuracy of the incident at Miletus. If Paul were in such haste, they ask, why delay his journey by stopping at Miletus?

If a father were traveling from one section of the country to another why should he linger between stations long enough to share a brief rendezvous with his children who perhaps are away at boarding school? To ask that is to answer it. I make no apology for the comparison. The relationship of pastor and people is not a far cry from that of parent and child. At its best it is one of the most beautiful associations under God's care.

The relationship of Paul and his Ephesian flock was one of such beauty. If ever the heart of a radiant fellowship is unveiled, it is disclosed to us in this twentieth chapter of Acts.

Paul feels this will be his last opportunity to instruct these elders of the church. Hence he speaks to them from his heart. He first tells them the way he declared the gospel when he had been with them earlier. He tells them the specific people to whom the gospel was directed. Finally, he reminds them of some of the differing facets of the gospel which he feels are vital.

We shall investigate these three points, approaching them in the form of three questions.

I

How did Paul preach the gospel at Ephesus? He answers this question in his opening remarks to the elders—"in public and in your homes" (NEB).

We do not have to read very far in the Gospels to observe that the ministry of our Lord was a public one. Often we find scenes like this: "A great multitude, hearing all that he did, came to him." (Mark 3:8.)

It would also be well to reflect upon the fact that the early church had its greatest day in the power of a mass movement. Luke writes, "Those who received his word were baptized and there were added that day about three thousand souls." (Acts 2:41.)

Mass evangelism is definitely a way of winning people to Christ and his church in the twentieth century. When hundreds of people band together in a concerted prayer effort it is not surprising that marvelous victories occur.

I have attended a number of large crusades. Often the preaching has been rather mediocre. The singing has not been of the finest caliber. Yet when the invitation to follow Christ or to rededicate one's life to discipleship was extended the power of the Spirit was evident. On occasions the results were amazing triumphs for the Kingdom. I have followed up some of these victories and I know them to be genuine.

I think there is little doubt but that the success of the Billy Graham revivals is largely due to concerted prayer.

This is certainly not to suggest that Mr. Graham is lacking in dedication. His devotion to Christ is not a matter of question. No more is this an insinuation that his team is not talented nor that his organization is not effective. But when he stands to preach, not only thousands present in the auditorium but literally millions across the world are lifting him to God on wings of prayer. No wonder his city-wide campaigns have proved helpful.

"I taught you . . . in your homes," said Paul. This is the personal touch. It is the most effective means of evangelism. This was true in the days when the church was young.

In my opinion it was in a home where the Spirit was received. There are those who believe that the Holy Spirit came first to the disciples in the Temple. "They were all together in one place," and some suggest that the Temple indeed was that place.

Nevertheless, the disciples were gathered in an upper room praying and waiting for the promised gift. I find it difficult to believe that this avowed assurance would have come to pass in a place that had not become warm with expectancy and hallowed by prayer. I think it is altogether probable that it was this Upper Room, this closet of commitment, where the Spirit made his initial entrance.

Not only was it in a home where the Spirit was received, but it was in a home where worship was conducted. The first Christian church was the home of John Mark's mother.

Just as we are told that Paul taught in public and in homes, so we read that the apostles did not cease teaching and preaching Jesus every day in the Temple and at home.

110

The "church in your house" is an expression that Paul used several times.

At least once each year in our church we have a family altar dedication service. When I am gone from my local congregation and preaching at special gatherings, I feel more and more impressed to encourage this particular devotion. Recently, after having answered such a public invitation, a young Baptist deacon gave me a glowing affirmation. "There is as much difference in our home since we began reading the Bible and praying together," he said, "as when we first began attending church."

The Christian home has no equal. There is no substitute for it. Church-related schools, sanctuary worship, Sunday morning classes in the main only complement the spiritual training in the home. We cannot expect our children to grasp in a limited time at different places what they are failing to learn constantly in the home.

II

To whom did Paul preach at Ephesus? "Both to Jews and to Greeks," he asserts. Paul felt constrained to preach to the Jews. Earlier he had gone to their synagogue at Ephesus and presented to them the claims of the Kingdom. Naturally, when he was treated in all ill fashion there, he had to withdraw for that particular season and share the gospel tidings elsewhere.

This seemed to be the constant fate of the gospel. It was proclaimed to those whose tradition seemed to speak of

111

immediate acceptance. Yet "he came unto his own home, and his own people received him not." (John 1:11.)

There are no sadder words found in the New Testament that our Lord's pathetic heart-cry over Jerusalem. "Oh, Jerusalem," he said. "How often have I longed to gather your children round me like a bird gathering her brood together under her wings—and you would never have it." (Matt. 23:37 Phillips.) Or our Lord's statement to the Jews as recorded in the fifth chapter of John: "You refuse to come to me that you may have life."

What we are attempting to say at this point is simply this: The Jews, those inside the church, were given precedence in the administration of the Word. The gospel "is the saving power of God for everyone who has faith," Paul wrote the Romans, but he adds "the Jew first." (Rom. 1:16 NEB.) That many of the Jews rejected the good news does not contradict the fact that they had it preached to them.

Those disciples closest to our Lord were Jews who dared believe and accept the gospel, then changed the world by its dispensation. So it is the same today! Revival must begin within the church before lives on the outside will be altered by its impact.

This has been true in regard to all of the mighty religious awakenings. Augustine's conversion to inner purity became the rally call of the fifth-century church. Luther's conversion to personal contact with God started the Reformation of the sixteenth century. Wesley's conversion from form to faith brought new life to the church of the eighteenth century and saved England from revolution.

"The creation waits with eager longing for the sons of God to be revealed." (Rom. 8:19 Moffatt.) This is true not in some distant tomorrow for now is the hour of need.

This leads us to observe that the Greeks, those outside the church, are needy children of his creation who are looking wistfully for abundant life. It is our sacred privilege and our divine commission to bring to them the tidings of great joy.

Jesus said, "You are the light of the world." After the darkness has been driven out of our own hearts, we are to shine before men so that they will no longer desire to live in the shadows. This is the twofold purpose of his reference to light: We are to have it—we are to share it. How easy it is for us to seek the blessing of salvation we desire only to hoard it for ourselves once we find it.

The church of Capernaum yielded to this temptation. How they must have thrilled at the marvelous results of our Lord's ministry in their midst. Here he taught and saved and healed and blessed. They would have kept him there if they could. But "I must tell the good news of the kingdom of God to other towns as well," he said. "That is my mission." (Luke 4:43 Phillips.) And it is ours.

> I love to tell the story,
>   For some have never heard
> The message of salvation
>   From God's own holy word.
>   —KATHERINE HANKEY

III

What did Paul preach at Ephesus? To be sure there were a number of things the devoted missionary proclaimed to his Ephesian flock that he considered vital. Let us look at four abiding essentials that he stressed.

Repentance and *faith* are both mentioned in the same breath. They needed to be declared then. They need to be asserted now. Salvation is impossible if these two elements are excluded.

Repentance was necessary for the Jew because of his willful rejection of Jesus. It was essential for the Greek because of his godless living. The Jew must repent for his indifference—the Greek for his ignorance. Of the two sins, the former is the greater. "This is the sentence of condemnation," said Jesus. "The Light has entered the world and yet men have preferred darkness." (John 3:19 Moffatt.)

It is imperative that we see the importance of this point. Jesus did not say, "You neglect to comprehend me." He said, "You refuse to come to me."

Let us not dare think that we in America can claim the lack of enlightenment in regard to this issue. The Bible is still our best seller. Thousands of churches by their very existence invite us to God. Daily newspaper devotionals, television broadcasts, and radio programs advocate the name of our Lord. Yet how many still prefer the darkness. Could the priest and Levite plead unawareness in failing to help one who was half dead? Jesus said they passed by on the other side when they saw him. Could the rich man pretend not to know about Lazarus when he lay at his gate too weak to move on? Could the servant that buried his thousand dollars excuse himself on the grounds of ignorance when his employer had entrusted to him his property. Their need is our need. We must repent.

Not only did Paul preach repentance to the Ephesians but he also proclaimed "faith in our Lord Jesus Christ." One must certainly repent of what he is and what he has done. But before salvation is his he must have confidence in who Christ is and what he has done to grant us this precious gift.

For the Jews this had to be faith not in their legal traditions nor in their ceremonies of ritual but in Jesus as Christ the Deliverer. For the Greeks this meant faith not in their pagan shrines of idolatry but in the Savior who had come to bring release and new life.

How was this great gift possible? First, life abundant was available because of Christ's atoning death. No longer was it necessary for man to seek a way of atonement for his failures and faults. The Cross bridged the chasm between man's longing and God's loving. Since the initiative had been taken by Christ, it was thus man's charge not to achieve but to believe.

Then the Christ life was within faith's reach of all men because of our Lord's resurrection. If the Cross was a bridge making possible the fellowship of God and man, then the empty tomb was a thoroughfare whose opening vistas and

115

widening horizons brought ever-increasing joy and certainty to those who walked with Christ.

Another facet of the gospel to which Paul gave attention while in Ephesus was *grace*. His only desire, he said, was to bear his testimony to the gospel of "God's grace."

How vague we are with our generalities. We scatter abroad such words as grace, thinking perhaps that everyone will know exactly what we mean or at least understand it in a fashion similar to our understanding of it. I fear I have been guilty of this. I was partially if not entirely cured, however, of the habit of cliché slinging while preaching in our overseas missions. Sometimes I would address people to whom the gospel message was almost completely new. They wondered what phrases like "being born anew" really meant. They wanted words like grace and salvation and faith and mercy explained.

It may be that we today need a fresh interpretation. Consider this word "grace" for instance. What does it mean? "The gospel of the grace of God"—that is the phrase Paul used as he preached in Ephesus. Dr. Jowett defined grace as God in action. I like that. I think Paul would have sanctioned that definition. He spoke in a similar vein to the Corinthians: "You know the grace of our Lord Jesus Christ, that though he was rich, yet for your sake he became poor." (II Cor. 8:9.) Later he said: "In his good pleasure God . . . called me through his grace." (Gal. 1:15 NEB.) So grace is God taking the initiative—God acting—God moving—God doing—for us.

116

Further, I do not think it would be presuming upon the apostle from Tarsus to say that he felt the greatest evidence of God's action is viewed at Calvary. The Ephesian people had heard their beloved pastor advocate such truth. "It is through the Son, at the cost of his own blood, that we are redeemed," Paul had said, "freely forgiven through that full and generous grace which has overflowed into our lives." (Eph. 1:7 Phillips.)

The last great essential to which we shall devote our interest is *giving*. Paul called upon the elders of Ephesus to remember these words of our Lord: "It is more blessed to give than to receive."

Now these words are not found in any of the Gospels. But we do not doubt that Jesus said them. In the first place, we believe Paul. In the second place, the words are so in keeping with the character of the Master. Just before, Paul had spoken a similar word on this subject of giving. "Feed the church of the Lord which he obtained with his own blood," he had admonished.

How may we give? How can we feed the church?

Well, of course, the elementary answer is we may give of our possessions. Let us not yawn when we speak of giving and commitment to the Lord in the same breath. Jesus said seven times more about money than he did any other subject.

I appreciated something a layman said in our church not long ago. We were engaged in a stewardship emphasis. A panel was chosen to answer the questions that members of

117

the congregation sent in. One of the queries asked was, "Why tithe?" "Why not give as the conscience directs?" The layman's answer was quite frank. "I am not sure what phase of conscience the one who asked this question is passing through," he said. "There was a time I dropped a dollar in the plate each week and my conscience never bothered me. I guess," he concluded, "it all depends on whether or not one's conscience has been touched by the Holy Spirit."

The church needs to be fed not only by material possessions but above all by spiritual witness. Our witness may be given by helpful deeds, loving words, or simply transformed lives. Either way, when the heart is committed, the service will come. Paul said of the Macedonians: "They gave according to their means . . . but first they gave themselves to the Lord."

I had an experience not long ago that was not unique, I am sure. I was visiting my brother who lives in a distant city. We were returning from a drive together and as we entered his apartment he took the mail from his box. I chanced to see a slip of paper that at once interested me. It was a card from his service station attendant. It said in effect that it was time for his car's oil to be changed and closed with a friendly invitation to drop by at his convenience. When I inquired about it, my brother answered that the station operator kept a record of the last oil change and always notified him in like fashion at about the time his car needed attention.

"My soul," I thought to myself, "if I were as concerned—

if I had a dozen laymen in my church as concerned—with saving souls as that man was concerned with selling oil, how the fires of revival would burn." I dare to suggest that if this were true of the pastors and their flocks our church would be gloriously fed.

XI
THE PERIL
OF POSTPONING

While Paul was talking about goodness, self-control and the judgment that is to come, Felix became alarmed, and said,

"You may go for the present. When I find a convenient moment I will send for you again." —ACTS 24:25 *Phillips*

Here is a sentence from W. R. Maltby that is well worth remembering. "In the Sermon on the Mount, Jesus promised his disciples three things—that they would be entirely fearless, absurdly happy, and that they would get

120

into trouble." To none of the disciples did this promise prove more valid than to Paul.

Was he fearless? Yes, he told the Ephesian elders: "The Holy Ghost witnesseth in every city, saying, that bonds and afflictions abide me. But none of these things move me." (Acts 20:23-24 KJV.)

Was he happy? It is doubtful if the Lord ever had a more radiant ambassador. There are so many instances of this. Read again his philosophy of the Kingdom as presented to the Romans: "The kingdom of God is . . . joy, inspired by the Holy Spirit." (Rom. 14:17 NEB.)

Was he ever in trouble? It would be better to ask was he ever out of trouble. Consider this testimony to the Corinthians:

> I have served . . . prison sentences!
> I have been beaten times without number.
> I have faced death again and again. . . .
> I have been stoned once.
> I have been shipwrecked three times. . . .
> I have known exhaustion, pain, long vigils, hunger and thirst, . . . cold and lack of clothing. (II Cor. 11:23-27 Phillips.)

Even as he converses with Felix at Caesarea, he is the governor's captive. He has actually been brought here as a prisoner to escape death at the hands of his enemies in Jerusalem. From trouble to trouble could very well be the caption for the life portrait of the evangelist.

Yet being a prisoner does not keep Paul from being a preacher. It is the content of his sermon to Felix, the response that the governor makes, and the resulting consequence that is the basis of our thinking here.

I

The first thing that Paul preached to Felix was *goodness*. The evangelist was declaring to the governor the need for a right relationship between man and God and between man and man.

Felix had heard his prisoner preach on this subject before. When Paul had first arrived at Caesarea, he had given this personal word: "I too endeavour to have a clear conscience before God and men all the time" (Acts 24:16 Moffatt).

Now someone might suggest that Felix was ignorant of the Christian attitude concerning the moral life. He could not be blamed for that which he knew so little about. There are, however, at least three bits of evidence that contradict this assumption.

The first is we are told that Felix had a rather accurate knowledge of the Way. No doubt this pertains to head rather than heart but it does suggest at least familiarity with the Christian movement.

The second is his wife Drusilla. Drusilla we know was a Jewess. She had deserted her husband, King Aziz of Emessa, for Felix. This is contrary to Jewish law. Now Luke tells us that as Paul preached to Felix the Roman procurator became alarmed. This alarm was caused by a deep sense of conviction. I think, too, Felix was fearful of the effect this sermon might have on his wife. Perhaps he even saw

122

the effect as the captive preacher seared her conscience. Be that as it may, she knew the law and no doubt she and her husband had discussed their illicit marriage many times.

The third evident point is that Paul did not simply have this one audience with the governor. It has already been pointed out that Felix had heard him before this particular meeting when he became alarmed. Luke says that he often sent for Paul after the scene we are now considering and conversed with him. Knowing the evangelist as we do and having seen the kind of preaching it took to arouse Felix, it is rather doubtful if Paul ever wandered too far from the subject at hand in his conferences with Felix.

The second theme to which Paul called the governor's attention was *self-control*. Before right relationships can be exercised with others a man must be right within—self-mastery, as Moffatt has it.

A grandmother and granddaughter read the Bible and prayed together each day. One of their favorite scripture selections was Christ's Sermon on the Mount, especially the first portion. One morning after they began with "Blessed are the poor in spirit," and concluded with, "Blessed are those who are persecuted for righteousness' sake," the elderly woman asked a rather deep question for her eight-year-old companion's consideration.

"My dear," she inquired, "if you could possess any single one of the eight beautitudes, which would you select?"

"Oh," said the little child, as if she had been considering the question for a very long while, "I would choose, 'Blessed are the pure in heart.' "

"Why would you pick that particular one," the old lady asked.

With eyes wondrously wise, her granddaughter answered, "If I had that one, I should have all the others, too."

The evangelist from Tarsus was proclaiming inner purity to a man who had stolen another man's wife. Had he been pure within, had he practiced self-control, this illicit relationship would have never developed. Had Felix now been pure of heart or yearning for this cleanliness, the alarm he felt because of the convincing presence of the Holy Spirit would have led to repentance and rebirth.

The third subject with which Paul dealt was *judgment*. We read that it was future judgment of which Paul spoke and no doubt this is true.

I wonder if this is not an almost entirely forgotten element in our contemporary preaching. Granted that our grandfathers painted pictures that were unnecessarily fantastic. Yet we have gone to the other extreme and speaking for myself, I cannot recall when last I heard a sermon on this text. "It is appointed for men to die once, and after that comes judgment." Do not forget that this theme is part of God's Word. Yes and it is part of our faith: "I believe . . . he shall come to judge the quick and the dead."

But there is also an ever-present judgment. There would soon be a day when Felix would be judged by Rome for his political tyranny. Still later a time would come when he would be judged by God for his spiritual negligence. We are, however, under the constant scrutiny of the Holy Spirit. Our Lord said: "When he [the Holy Spirit] comes, he will convince the world of the meaning of sin, of true goodness and of judgment. He will expose their sin because they do not believe in me." (John 16:8-9 Phillips.)

Thus did the Holy Spirit, through the preaching of Paul, judge Felix.

A missionary, home on furlough, told me of a conversation he had with a man who shared his seat on an airplane flight. Their communion became quite intimate. I think my friend felt that this man was eager for help. "I am living in adultery," he confided. Then he added, "I talked to my minister about it and he made me feel so good." Well that minister was no spiritual descendent of Paul. We must remember that if the Spirit judges others through our ministrations, he continually judges his ministers. When I recall the statement of the man to my missionary friend, I agree with Simon Peter—"It is time for the Judgment to begin with the household of God" (I Pet. 4:17 Moffatt).

II

What response did the governor make to the tidings Paul declared? He became alarmed and said, "You may go for the present. When I find a convenient moment I will send for you again." (Phillips.) Felix postponed the decision to receive the purity of heart about which Paul had been speaking. Why did he do it?

I think at least three reasons must be given for his procrastination.

First, Felix was *mentally hesitant*. I know Luke tells us

125

that he was well informed about the Christian movement. But, to use the excellent word picture of Theodore Ferris, he was one of that vast company who, "like the humming-bird, . . . hover above the nectar of life, but . . . never come to rest in the real richness of it."

There can be little doubt but that he was interested. Had he not been concerned he would not have sent for Paul time after time during the two years the evangelist was his prisoner.

Perhaps he felt he could by intellectual discernment find the peace about which Paul preached.

I visited one not long ago who had almost reached the summit of the hill. His minister and I sought by gentle persuasion to lead him to the moment of supreme commitment. We endeavored to explain to him as simply as if he had been a small child the way through the gates of new life. At length, with a puzzled expression he closed the interview.

"I do not understand," he said sadly. "I am sorry but I just do not understand."

How marvelous that our Lord does not require that we understand our way in. He did not say, "Whoever does not perceive the Kingdom like a scholar shall not enter it." Rather he said, "Whoever does not receive the kingdom of God like a child shall not enter it."

Second, Felix was *materially anxious*. This has been a barrier which has kept many from fellowship with Christ.

How enthusiastic was that young man who came to

Christ in Judea. Mark says he ran to Jesus. How earnest he was. We read that he knelt before Jesus. How reverent he was. When the Master discussed with him six ethical commandments touching his relationship to his associates, he answered that he had kept them all. But when Jesus told him to sell what he had and share it with those who had not, we read that he went away with a heavy heart. He was more eager to keep his material wealth than he was to know the greater wealth of Christ's abiding presence.

Luke informs us that Felix hoped Paul would give him money. Perhaps he felt a man of Paul's intellect should bring a sizable bribe. Releasing a captive on such grounds was of course forbidden by law. But regulations meant little to a man of so little integrity as Felix.

Third, Felix was *morally corrupt*. It has already been pointed out that he may have become alarmed in part as Paul preached because he feared the effect the sermon might have on Drusilla. He did not want Drusilla to leave him. And he had no intention of leaving her.

There is a moving scene in *Hamlet* where the guilt-conscious Claudius considers prayer as a means of receiving forgiveness for his crime.

> . . . Oh, what form of prayer
> Can serve my turn? "Forgive me my foul murder?"
> That cannot be; since I am still possess'd
> Of those effects for which I did the murder,
> My crown, mine own ambition and my queen.
> May one be pardon'd and retain the offense?

Dissolving his marriage would not have brought cleansing to Claudius. No more to Felix. Additional wrong never makes right. There was but one way for either man to drive the shadows from his soul, and that was not to order his wife's departure but to invite his Savior's entrance. This Felix refused to do. Again, the reason for his alarm was not only because he was convicted of his sin but because he was afraid he might lose the fruit of his vice.

III

What was the consequence of the governor's procrastinating? Look first at the personal effect.

We have no reason to believe that Felix's postponement was anything but permanent. There may have been times in the two-year interval while Paul was his prisoner that the governor looked rather wistfully toward the high road he had missed. But if he ever became a Christian convert, Paul never mentioned it to Luke. We believe that he would have hardly kept it a secret. Felix was a man of high station and the evangelist labored long with him. Though it is tragic, yet it seems true that the governor never found life at its radiant best.

Look next at the social result. What an influence this man might have wielded for the cause of Christ. He might have been the very one to have guided his back-slidden wife into the sunlight where she had walked as a girl. He could have been a power for the Master in his office and the Lord sorely needed his witness in such a position.

128

The Peril of Postponing

Two pictures are before the vision of my imagination. One is of an aged infidel living on a back street in the city of Rome. Years ago he was called back to the capital for the mismanagement of one of the empire's provinces. Long since his wife has left him. He seldom journeys out where the crowds gather, for fingers point and men sneer and children laugh. Disgraced by Nero, he has become a bitter and cynical recluse.

The other picture is of a devoted Christian who lives in the highlands of Judea. Though he is very old, his small cottage knows little solitude. He and his faithful wife are loyal hosts to the wayfarers who frequent their welcome. Children are their constant guests. The little ones love to hear the old man's stories. There is one he tells repeatedly. It concerns his early life when he was a Roman procurator. It seems a prisoner was brought under his jurisdiction—a prisoner who years before had made a marvelous discovery. The prisoner disclosed that discovery to the governor, and he too found the pearl of great price.

What makes the difference in these two pictures? There is but one answer. Christ!

XII
MAGNIFICENT MADNESS

As he [Paul] thus made his defense, Festus said with a loud voice, "Paul, you are mad." —ACTS 26:24

Nineteenth-century critics of Paul were varied and numerous. Starting out as diversified attacks against his theology, these assaults became all but concentrated warfare. This active aggression swept into the twentieth century and many came to disbelieve in the greatness of the evangelist from Tarsus.

130

Paul had an epileptic fit on the Damascus road says one critic. One is tempted to answer that if that is so then the church today needs an epidemic of epilepsy. There was no vision of Christ, says another censor, he merely suffered a sunstroke. Again one is tempted to answer that the difference in his life was such that a similar heat wave would be most beneficial to the Christian community.

The critics of the missionary were many during his life. In this particular scene, Paul is declaring his faith at Caesarea a short while before sailing to Rome. He has all but declared the entire gospel: forgiveness, salvation, the Atonement, and Resurrection. But suddenly his sermon is cut short by the governor's interruption. "Paul, you are mad," Festus asserts. "Your great learning is turning you mad."

Why did Festus accuse the evangelist of insanity?

I

Festus thought Paul was mad because in preaching the gospel to the governor, Paul was speaking of something that Festus knew little or nothing about.

Once Jesus was preaching in a certain city and four men sought to bring a paralyzed man to him to be healed. The crowd was so large that the men could not get their friend to Jesus through the usual entrance. Luke informs us that they went up on the roof and let him down through the tiles. Jesus not only healed the man but saved him. Then

Luke gives us this significant word: "Amazement seized them all, and they glorified God and were filled with awe, saying, 'We have seen strange things today.'"

Any sight can be strange if you are not accustomed to seeing it. And any spokesman could be classified as crazy if he speaks on some subject totally foreign to you.

One can imagine the bewilderment on the face of Festus when Paul utters this sort of phrase, "Christ being the first to rise from the dead." To believe in the living Christ, one must experience the living Christ. This was the reason Paul was preaching to this gathering at Caesarea.

Festus, however, did not allow himself to come under the spirit of conviction which had so laid seige to the soul of Felix. He checks Paul and he does so vehemently. Therefore we have to conclude that Festus in this particular instance did not come to know Christ because he simply had no intention of doing so. One must, you understand, have the determination before he can possess the dedication. Our Lord said: "If anyone wants to do God's will, he will know." (John 7:17 Phillips.)

The desire to know is the first step toward spiritual certainty. Before the Master transformed the woman of Sychar into a citywide evangelist, he had to first create within her a curiosity for the highest. How surprised she was when he spoke to her, a despised woman of Samaria, and requested a cup of water.

"How can you, a Jew, ask for a drink from me, a woman of Samaria?" she inquired. With marvelous insight, Jesus answered, "If you knew what God can give, and if you knew who it is that said to you, 'Give me a drink,' you would have asked him, and he would have given you living water!" (John 4:9-10 Phillips.)

Thus wishing to know both gift and giver it is not long until she finds both and with them a new purpose for living.

I have seen people converted at our church altars. Some were so wonderfully transformed that this new experience in Christ became their only reason for existence. Occasionally I have noticed that a few of the staid members were critical. "Off the deep end," is a statement the ear catches once in a while.

But if these people are off the deep end, then so were the disciples after Pentecost. So was Paul after Damascus. So was Wesley after Aldersgate. I am suggesting that a man is not really normal until he is really Christian. As another has indicated, "Many of us have been subnormal so long that when we actually see a man who is normal we think he is abnormal."

Let this word be of encouragement to you. If knowing Christ and seeking by every opportunity to make Him known to others is madness, then it is magnificent madness. One is all but tempted to say, speaking in this context, that it is ideal to be insane.

Too, you will be in good company. For mad is not only what they called Paul; it is what they called Paul's Lord. At one time we are told that Jesus' own family thought he was out of his mind.

133

II

Festus thought Paul was mad because the evangelist was so tremendously enthusiastic concerning the tidings he delivered. Here was a preacher who had been shut up in prison for many months. Yet he was still so eager in his faith that he dared call a king and governor to repentance. This enthusiasm was born of two things. First, it came from Paul's personal experience.

Agrippa and his sister, Bernice, had come to pay their respects to the Roman representative. While they were visiting Festus, the governor invited them to hear his prisoner, explaining to them that the chief charge the Jews brought against Paul was his insistence that Christ had risen from the dead. This interested Agrippa and a day was set for the hearing.

When Paul made his defense, prisoner though he was, he became more defender than defendant. His appeal was not so much an answer to his critics as it was a declaration of his faith. His defense builds to a climax with the testimony of his own conversion: "I saw on the way a light from heaven."

This light chased out all the shadows of his misguided actions. This light brought to him the glorious dawn of an unsurpassed ministry which would take him across the Roman Empire for Christ. This light would shine in his heart and dispel the gloom of dangerous foes and dungeon cells.

There were many thrilling adventures Paul shared with

his Lord. But the flaming heart was first kindled on the Damascus road. His consecration began where all consecration begins—with conversion. But if the enthusiasm of Paul was born of his personal experience *with* Christ, the fire was continually fanned by his victorious witness *about* Christ.

Possibly the king and governor were familiar with Jewish priests whether they had heard them or not. But this rabbi was something entirely new for them. How they must have wondered as they listened to this ardent advocate preach with such power. His words, however, were beyond them —suffering Lord, risen Savior, Light to Jew and Gentile. "Madness," cries Festus.

The climax to his sermon in the courtroom at Caesarea does not conclude with his conversion. It extends to his witness. "I was not disobedient to the heavenly vision," he asserts, "but declared first to those at Damascus, then at Jerusalem and throughout all the country of Judea, and also to the Gentiles, that they should repent and turn to God."

In a moment he is interrupted by Festus but not before he outlines the basis of his transforming theology. "Christ should suffer," he said, "that he should be the first to rise from the dead, and so proclaim the message of light both to our people and to the Gentiles" (Acts 26:23 Phillips.)

III

Let us look at these three vital elements that comprise Paul's witness at Caesarea.

1. "Christ must suffer." Indeed the *Crucifixion* was the very soul of the evangelist's message. Certainly Festus thought Paul was mad. The evangelist himself said that the preaching of the cross is "nonsense to those who are involved in this dying world." (I Cor. 1:18 Phillips.)

"But to us who are being saved," Paul adds, "it is [nothing less than] the power of God." So! the preaching of the Cross calls for the listener to respond with derision or dedication. Paul had seen men sneer at it but he had also seen men saved by it.

Do not many of us belong to one of these two camps? We jeer at its folly or we join in its power. We scoff or salute. We mock or we magnify.

Years ago while I was preaching in Malaya I came to know a group of men who magnified the Cross more, I think, than any I have ever seen. Their leader was a converted gambler named Kow Chiang. These men called themselves "The Cross-Sharers." What powerful Christians they were! The theme of their witness was not so much the joy of belonging to a club but the victory of bearing a cross.

2. "He should be the first to rise from the dead." The *Resurrection* was stressed before Festus called a halt to Paul's sermon. Paul had been ridiculed before for declaring this fact. When he proclaimed the Resurrection in Athens we recall that some of the people mocked.

Even when our Lord was risen and appeared to the disciples on the mountain we are told that some doubted. When, however, they became certain that he was alive,

136

they were utterly transformed. They went forth, Mark says, and preached everywhere. It was the touch of the deathless Christ that changed Saul into Paul.

"Did not our hearts burn within us while he talked to us?" Cleopas and his wife asked each other after Christ had journeyed with them to Emmaus. A corpse cannot set two hearts ablaze.

3. "He would proclaim [the message of] light both to [our] people and to the Gentiles." The Crucifixion he endured, the Resurrection he achieved, and now the *regeneration* he offered completed Paul's sermon in the courtroom.

We are not sure how much knowledge Agrippa and Festus possessed regarding Jewish worship. It is doubtful if their understanding of it was detailed. Yet even a casual observer would hardly describe the Temple by using the word light.

Several years ago I visited in the Middle East. I walked through some of the cities and villages where the Master had journeyed in the long ago. In the course of this tour I gave considerable attention to the temples. I entered the incense filled corridors and the darkened halls. I recall noting in my diary these words: "How very unlike our Lord."

How often he preached in the open air, in the hills and by the sea. No dark, drab, dingy religion was his. And this was the gospel he lived and shared. Light!

> The people who walked in darkness
> have seen a great light.

He was that Light. "He who follows me will not walk in darkness, but will have the light of life." His way was a lighted way.

This lighted way, Paul declares, is for all men: "To the people [that is the Jews] and to the Gentiles," he says. So with this description of the Christian religion Paul is forced to conclude his defense. "Light," says the evangelist. "Madness," says the governor.

The interruption of Festus ends the sermon. The courtroom is cleared. The governor and the king walk out together. "This man," they agreed, "is doing nothing to deserve death or imprisonment." Then Agrippa said to Festus, "This man could have been set free if he had not appealed to Caesar."

Mad perhaps but not a criminal they decided. And yet this simple statement by Agrippa but reminded the governor of what he had already decided. What hope could a man have in appealing to the emperor? How could a man whose God was a crucified rabbi expect liberty from a man who himself claimed to be God? Paul's words, thought Festus, bear witness that he is mad. But appealing to Caesar—that is the supreme evidence of insanity. Death could only be the result.

But it was not freedom that the evangelist sought. It was the opportunity to carry the gospel to Rome. And death would come eventually because of it. But no matter, if only he could present the claims of Christ in that great wicked city.

Little wonder Festus thought Paul was mad. He proclaimed strange things that startled the governor. He did it with amazing fervor. And now he seemed to be actually in haste to die. This was the supreme mark of madness—the willingness to face death.

There is a rather remarkable sentence in the Letter of Paul to the Philippians. I never read it that it doesn't serve as a battle cry to my soul. "You have been granted the privilege not only of believing in Christ," said the evangelist, "but also of suffering for him. You and I are engaged in the same contest." (Phil. 1:29-30 NEB.)

There is something tremendous in those words. He seems to say that in reality the Cross is our greatest gain, our most blessed prize. The highest privilege is to endure pain for the sake of Christ.

The finest book I have read this year is *Through the Valley of the Kwai.* Ernest Gordon, who was himself a prisoner in the death camp of Thailand, has given us an amazing witness of spiritual heroism which he and his fellow prisoners sustained in the grip of the Japanese.

He relates that at the end of a day's toil one of the Japanese guards declared a shovel was missing. When he demanded that the guilty one in the work detail step forward, none of the men complied. The guard responded by shrieking: "All die! All die!" He then put the rifle to his shoulder and prepared to shoot. At once a Scotch soldier moved forward and admitted taking the shovel. He was brutally kicked and beaten and killed on the spot. But

139

when the men returned to the camp and the tools were counted, there was no shovel missing.

Mad? Yes, like Christ when he climbed to Golgotha and Paul when he sailed to Rome. Like all Christians who for love's sake face Calvary.